2

American-Japanese Relations
In A Changing Era

2

THE WASHINGTON PAPERS

American-Japanese Relations In A Changing Era

Robert Scalapino

The Center for Strategic and International Studies
Georgetown University, Washington, D.C.

THE LIBRARY PRESS
NEW YORK
1972

Copyright © 1972 by
The Center for Strategic and International Studies,
Georgetown University

Library of Congress Catalog Card Number:
72-6270

International Standard Book Number:
0-912050-34-9

I am very grateful to Ralph N. Clough, Donald C. Hellman and James W. Morley for their critical reading and comments upon this monograph. The responsibility for the contents is naturally mine.

CONTENTS

BACKGROUND

S hortly after World War I, a significant change took place in the structure of Pacific-Asian international politics. The Anglo-Japanese alliance which had underwritten Japanese policy for two decades was scrapped. Substituted were a series of multilateral agreements among the major Pacific powers, codified in treaty form at the Washington Conference of 1921-1922. These agreements were centrally concerned with peaceful coexistence and disarmament, issues as vital then as now. Mutual consultation among the big powers of that era was pledged in the event of violations. (The major powers were all European, except for the United States and Japan.)

Thus was the first experiment in a loosely-knit multipolarism launched in East Asia. It was accompanied, moreover, by the abandonment of a bilateral alliance that had previously been the linch-pin of Far Eastern international relations. Unfortunately, history would reveal that neither Japan nor her Pacific-Asian neighbors were to benefit from the change. The Washington treaties rested essentially upon the thesis that a broad community of interests existed among highly diverse nations. When that premise later proved false, there were no enforcement mechanisms that could uphold the peace. Moral suasion was the only available weapon in a rapidly disintegrating world, and it proved wholly insufficient.

Are we witnessing a parallel development today? Is the American-Japanese alliance, having exercised a major influence for twenty years, now to be replaced by a new loosely-knit multipolar structure? Before commenting upon the applicability or inapplicability of the past, we should note that the events of 1921-1922 are not the only historical milestones brought to memory by current trends. One might also recall the finale of the Russo-Japanese war, in 1905. Victory in that war altered markedly the image of Japan both in Asia and in America. Previously, Japan had been seen as a weak, emerging nation but one with remarkable capacities for adaptation and growth. Hence, the image was a favorable one, especially in the United States. After it had humbled the great Russian empire, changes took place and Japan's prestige rose sharply among Asian elites, particularly those aspiring to independence and power. In some Western quarters, however, the Japanese image became a less attractive one – that of the brash adolescent; abrasive, demanding, and even competitive.

The new image was duly reflected in certain American attitudes and policies. Indeed, friction between the United States and Japan has sometimes been dated from the Portsmouth treaty of August 1905. In this, there is more than a touch of irony, because only a few years earlier, the United States had exhibited strong paternalist feelings toward Japan, and President Theodore Roosevelt had looked forward to the role of mediator of the conflict with pride and expectation.

Or should one seek an analogy from a later, more ominous period? The Manchurian Incident of September 1931 represented yet another point of decisive change. The United States, deep in the midst of an economic crisis and strongly committed to an isolationist course, lacked the will and power to exercise a constructive influence on the international scene. World trends and domestic problems, meanwhile, combined to cause Japan to break away from earlier multilateral commitments and seek an autonomous foreign policy. Its primary goals were to end the Western domination of Asia and to create a sphere of coprosperity and coexistence in the Far East under Japanese hegemony. Both economic and political-military power were directed to these ends with striking initial results. Yet a collision course between Japan and the United States loomed ahead.

It is tempting to use any one of these episodes to explain contemporary trends. That temptation must be resisted. There are important lessons to be learned and remembered from the past, as even our brief recitation of three events should suggest. However, to read the past into the present in any crude or undifferentiated fashion is foolish. Events taken from the history of modern Asian international relations can be used to illustrate the periodic reoccurrence of certain developments that alter national attitudes and policies. They may lead to crisis or conflict. Yet, even when current developments show close similarities to history, the total mix of factors, both domestic and international, can easily cause dramatically different responses, or consequences.

The Japan of 1972 is not the Japan of 1902, 1922, or 1932. Similarly, both the United States and East Asia have undergone massive changes in recent decades. Despite the heightened appeal of domestic priorities and the considerable disillusionment with internationalism, the American nation is not likely to revert completely to the simplistic mood and policies of the isolationist era. Our stake in the peace and prosperity of the Pacific-Asian region is too great.

Meanwhile, the continent of Asia is no longer the vacuum of power it was in the period immediately before World War

II. Indeed, the two most formidable military powers of East Asia are continental nations – the U.S.S.R. and the People's Republic of China. Currently in hostile confrontation with each other, each is still expanding its military arsenal. With the exception of the Soviet Union, the European powers play a negligible role in Asia today. The age of European colonialism is over: the primary actors in the international politics of Asia during the 1970s will be those nations located in the Pacific-Asian region.

The Asian Context of American-Japanese Relations

It is thus essential to place American-Japanese relations in their Asian setting. What is the broader context in which our bilateral relations will operate in the era ahead? The conventional wisdom can be set forth easily: the age of *pax Americana* in East Asia is coming to an end. In its place, a loosely-knit multipolar power structure is emerging, with the United States, the Soviet Union, China, Japan, and possibly India as the principal figures. In some quarters, this new structure is seen as composed of states whose concept of national interest will place them roughly equidistant from each other. Consequently, it is argued, actions will be taken in a highly pragmatic fashion, wholly or largely separate from commitments of "principle." Thus, the end of ideology in the international realm is being widely predicted. The Cold War, it is proclaimed, is over, with Communist versus non-Communist lines now gone, and total Soviet versus American confrontation no longer meaningful.

There is a considerable element of truth in this analysis. But there are also elements of distortion and error, some of them very serious. Whatever the future may hold, the present is not one of equidistant multipolarism in Asia, nor is that likely to emerge in the near future. On the contrary, bilateral relations between the major actors will vary greatly in scope, intensity, and international significance. Such relations, of course, will be influenced by the total network of contacts which each state establishes, but they will not be superceded soon by an international system resting primarily upon multilateral relationships. In the Pacific-Asian region at least, we are still a considerable distance from a broader community of any type. The massive differences in culture, level of development, and socio-political institutions have even inhibited the nation-building process as well as affective bilateralism in many cases. They make the far more ambitious goal of an international community truly remote.

Nor can ideology be dismissed out of hand. Ideological factors have rarely proven to be the primary determinant in any nation's foreign policy, as Soviet policies in the age of the Comintern should have taught us. Nevertheless, the major Communist states are likely to continue and even expand a three-dimensional approach to their foreign relations: state to state; people to people; and comrade to comrade. The precise mix among these will vary with time, place, and circumstances. Within people-to-people and comrade-to-comrade relations, however, the ideological element will be clearly present and on occasion as highly important in the future as it has been in the past. Nor should the ideological quotient in foreign policy be limited to the actions and attitudes of Communist states. Has it been, or will it be an insignificant factor in the policies and attitudes of the United States? In sum, differing perceptions of a desirable world order derived from different ideologies will continue to have important effects on the behavior of most major states.

The Sino-Soviet cleavage, together with the variations among East European Communist states, which have been developing since 1945, have indeed altered the structure of international politics characteristic of the late 1940s. One cannot speak of a coherent Communist bloc, as everyone knows. The relations among Communist states now closely resemble the relations among non-Communist states in many respects, with the full political continuum of alliance, neutrality, and enmity represented, together with various types of "neo-colonialism."

Note, for example, the current relations among the Communist states and parties of Asia. The confrontation between the two Communist giants dominates the international policies of each. That struggle, moreover, has been made the more bitter by their efforts to share (or, more accurately, to control) a common ideology. The need to claim the banners of orthodoxy and struggle against heresy affects both the style of disputation and its intensity.

The Russians were reportedly driven to threaten nuclear war in an effort to get Peking to the bargaining table. They keep approximately one million men on the lengthy Sino-Soviet frontier, together with a full range of sophisticated military equipment. The Chinese have responded with an all-out commitment to the acquisition of nuclear weapons irrespective of costs (although it should be carefully noted that this commitment *preceded* the Sino-Soviet conflict, and was one of the causes for it). The Chinese seek a credible nuclear deterrent, and are enroute to becoming a major military power, both in the nuclear and in the conventional fields.

On the political front, the Soviet Union, bitter foe of John Foster Dulles during his lifetime, has now become his most apt pupil. Moscow is building a containment policy toward China that dwarfs the containment policy initiated by the United States a few decades ago — and without abandoning her competitive stance vis-à-vis America. The Soviet alliance with India, coupled with its extensive pledges to Bangla Desh, comprises the southern portion of that containment. Russian overtures to almost all of the Southeast Asian states (including the Lon Nol government of Cambodia) aim at a buffer against China on her southeastern flank – albeit with limited results thus far. Even toward her historic enemy, Japan, Russia has recently sought to initiate a new era of amity and cooperation. This, together with the firm support of (and control over) the People's Republic of Mongolia, makes up the Soviet Union's current "northern strategy" and completes the containment arc. Interestingly, the effort to contain China has moved the Soviet Union in the general direction of becoming a status-quo power, operating with ever greater reliance on state-to-state relations.

In pursuing its new policies, however, Moscow has not ignored its relations with the Asian Communist parties, in or out of power. Once, only a few years ago, all seemed lost on this front. At the end of the Khrushchev era, Peking was in the ascendancy almost everywhere within the Asian Communist movement, with only Mongolia serving as a bastion of Soviet strength. At present, however, in addition to retaining their dominant position in Mongolia, the Russians have seemingly strengthened their influence in North Vietnam by virtue of massive military assistance and Hanoi's unhappiness over recent Chinese moves toward the United States, although the extent of that influence, and its implications, remain unclear. Compared to the Khrushchev era, the Soviet Union has even improved its relations with North Korea, which has generally exhibited an affinity for Chinese policies in recent years (except for a period of estrangement at the height of the Cultural Revolution) and which even now is seeking to adapt Peking's foreign policies to its relations with Japan and the United States. In considerable measure, this is because P'yŏngyang continues to be strongly dependent upon the Russians for both military and technical assistance.

Meanwhile, Moscow has largely mended its earlier rift with

the Japanese Communist party, which is bitterly anti-Mao at present. It has also strengthened its position with the right wing Indian Communists, and fought vigorously to oust the Chinese from positions of influence in certain other Communist movements, among them those of Indonesia, Ceylon and Pakistan.

The leaders of the Chinese People's Republic have not witnessed these developments passively. The events of 1968-1969 provided a climax to the Sino-Soviet quarrel, and profoundly altered the immediate course of China's foreign policy. The Soviet invasion of Czechoslovakia, followed swiftly by the veiled threat of a nuclear strike against China, evoked a new ordering of priorities in Peking's foreign policies and a major shift in tactics. The Chinese, or at least Mao Tse-tung and Chou En-lai, now saw the Soviet Union as the most threatening force, hence the primary opponent of the immediate future. But they also viewed the problem of Japan as extremely serious, particularly since the signs pointed to the possibility that Japan would assume a position of major responsibility for the integrity of South Korea and Taiwan as the United States reduced its commitments in northeast Asia. Would significant political and military components be added to Japan's great economic power throughout the region?

The goals of Chinese foreign policy thus became twofold. The first was to thwart Soviet containment efforts and to achieve as quickly as possible meaningful deterrents, both military and political, against all possible Soviet moves. The second was to contain Japan, blocking any effort to transfer responsibilities previously American to Japanese shoulders, and for these and other purposes, to weaken the American-Japanese alliance.

Toward these ends, China first ended the isolation that had reached its extreme point at the height of the Cultural

Revolution when active relations were broken off with almost every nation in the world. She then indicated an interest in entering the United Nations, a body shunned and reviled throughout much of the 1960s. But most important, Peking signaled a desire to enter into a new relation with the United States, one that would at once provide greater flexibility in meeting the Soviet challenge and shake previously established relations among the non-Communist Pacific-Asian states.

On balance, China has reason to be pleased with the initial results of its new policies. Relations have not only been reestablished with all states where ties had been disrupted during the Cultural Revolution, but have been established with a sizeable number of additional states, including some important ones. China's entry into the United Nations — largely on her terms — constituted another important gain. Correctly or not, Peking now believes that the Taiwan issue is going her way. In any case, there can be little doubt that relations between the United States and each of its Northeast Asian allies have become troubled and uncertain. While this development is by no means entirely due to the new American-Chinese détente, both the substance of the new "understanding" and the style with which it was executed have contributed to uneasiness in diverse quarters. Meanwhile, Japan has not moved in the direction of picking up earlier American commitments. On the contrary, the current Japanese mood is still one of a low military and political posture, as we shall see, and China's heavy propaganda barrage against "Japanese militarism" may have been a contributory factor.

Yet a price has been paid for these gains. China's revolutionary credibility appears to have suffered abroad, adding further divisions and disillusionment to the already fragmented ranks of international radicalism. Are the Chinese

Communists more than Chinese nationalists, and nationalists determined to play the big-power game, despite Chou En-lai's vehement denials? Recent Chinese policies appear to have troubled the North Vietnamese in particular, although the North Koreans have rallied to the new line and are experimenting with it themselves.

To the problems of political credibility must be added the more serious ones of military credibility. Despite all of its verbal support for Pakistan and the degree to which it staked its prestige on a Soviet-Indian defeat over the Bangla Desh issue, Peking could not influence the outcome, either militarily or politically. Indeed, Soviet sources boasted that the Chinese were unable even to move their forces toward the South Asian frontiers because of China's domestic situation. China's shadow does fall across much of Asia, particularly across those small states that border that mammoth society. That shadow may grow longer, moreover, as China's nuclear arsenal increases and her conventional forces are selectively modernized. Until a successful transition has been made into the post-Maoist era, however, and political instability has been prevented or contained, the political and military credibility of China will remain in some doubt. "Who is China?" and "What will China be?" are still highly legitimate questions.

Despite this disability, however, China's political reach in Asia at present is considerable; far beyond her economic or military power. In part, this is a product of her sheer size — of the psychological advantage of being the most populous state in the world and of commanding such a huge part of East Asia. Factors both of culture and of political tactics must also be acknowledged. Setbacks notwithstanding, the Chinese People's Republic continues to have a major influence upon Asian Communism. Where there are ethnic Chinese involved in the movement, as in Thailand, Malaysia,

Singapore, and Sarawak, such influence flows naturally. Meanwhile, the struggle over Indochina continues, with Peking seeking to preside over an Indochinese united front, and playing permanent host to one of its key symbols, Sihanouk. Sihanouk, however, is not China's only house guest. Certain Burmese and Indonesian Communist leaders have acquired semipermanent residence in Peking; a token of China's continuing revolutionary commitments and a warning to the governments concerned that alternate channels of support exist.

Peking's ties in Asia, however, extend well beyond the Communist movement. As we shall see, they now reach deeply into the Liberal Democratic Party of Japan, not as a result of ideological affinity but out of economic and political considerations. On the rim of South Asia, moreover, agreements with China represent both insurance and a counterpoint to Soviet or Indian influence in such states as Afghanistan, Pakistan, and Nepal. And nearly everywhere Peking's people-to-people diplomacy is on the upswing. If governments cannot be reached, they can be bypassed or challenged via this route.

It remains to look beyond the Russian and Chinese roles in contemporary Asia, and focus briefly upon changes in the American role. Unquestionably, the central question throughout East Asia revolves around the real meaning of recent changes in the Far Eastern policies of the United States, and their implications for the future. The general trend seems clear: after more than two decades of heavy and largely unilateral efforts to uphold the security and to advance the economic development of select Asian states, the United States has demanded that these responsibilities be shared by our various allies. At the same time, the United States has indicated to all opponents its willingness to enter into serious discussions on a wide range of issues, looking toward some "normalization" of relations and a reduction of tension.

These two broad goals, namely, mutually shared responsibilities among allied states and negotiation rather than confrontation with opponents, constitute the essence of the Nixon Doctrine in its original enunciation at Guam and its subsequent elaboration through application. In military terms, the objective is to make all states with which the United States is aligned wholly responsible for keeping internal order and responsible also for the primary role in their defense against externally directed attack, especially in cases of ground warfare. Through its strategic weapons the United States will seek to provide a sufficient deterrent to prevent direct major power intervention, and under certain conditions will furnish air and sea support for a beleaguered ally. American ground forces, however, will no longer be available (South Korea for the time being excepted). Regional defense arrangements among the countries immediately concerned are to be encouraged. Meanwhile, in-depth discussions with all major powers of the Pacific-Asian area are to be initiated with respect to the full range of military issues including nuclear weapon control, balanced reduction of arms, and limitations upon military assistance to client states.

In political terms, the Nixon Doctrine relies centrally upon a balance-of-power principle for the Pacific-Asian region, accepting the need for a differentiated treatment of allies and opponents, and seeking to retain in modified form the alliance structure previously constructed. Its ideal is a shared partnership, with a much higher degree of reciprocity among allies, and with elements of multilateralism gradually augmenting bilateral relations. Meanwhile, relations with opponents are to focus upon such basic tasks as defining the essential requirements of peaceful coexistence, probing the possibilities of weapons control and reduction, and exploring the means of more effective communications, both to forward the negotiations process and to reduce the risks of miscalculation.

On the economic front, the new policies are also broadly dedicated to a greater sharing of responsibilities and mutuality of treatment. As is well known, the serious crisis in the economic relations of the "advanced" nations and the rising economic problems within the American domestic scene were closely interrelated. And both reflected in large measure the intolerable burdens upon the United States engendered by the old international economic and political order, together with the grave deficiencies in the management of the American economy itself.

Due to the urgency of the situation and earlier evidence of strong reluctance on the part of foreign states to change their policies, the United states underwrote its demands for remedial actions by unilateral measures that forced a showdown. Both the short-range results and the shock were substantial. Meanwhile, with respect to the so-called "North-South" problem, or the issue of economic relations between the advanced states and the LDC (late-developing countries), once again, the Nixon Doctrine promotes expanded commitments from Japan and West Europe, as well as a heightened emphasis upon private investment, aid through such channels as the International Monetary Fund and the World Bank, and consortium arrangements. It also stresses the need for recipient nations to establish the bonafides of their intentions via the creation of practical programs and a reordering of priorities.

When the broad goals and methods of the Nixon Doctrine are spelled out in these terms, they evoke general acceptance if not enthusiastic support from those nations that have been closely associated with the United States in Asia. The troublesome issues, however, go beyond the acceptance or rejection of the basic principles. They relate to four far-reaching concerns: Can the manner in which these new policies are enunciated and the timing of their application be attuned to the existing international environment, and particularly to the essential requirements of those who have committed themselves in the past to American leadership, not merely to the domestic political situation in the United States? Can the Nixon Doctrine resolve certain internal contradictions implicit within it, opting for an internationalist approach to the issues it addresses rather than an essentially nationalist one? Can the Nixon Doctrine be sustained in the United States itself, stemming the neo-isolationist tide that appears to be running so strongly throughout the grass-roots of American society? And most important, can the Nixon Doctrine work when challenged militarily or otherwise by determined opponents?

Every foreign policy has its costs, and the costs to date of the new Asian policy of the United States relate primarily to our credibility with allies. This problem has manifested itself throughout the Asian area, but it is naturally most acute in South Korea, Taiwan, Japan, Indochina, and Thailand. Verbal reassurances, however sincere and closely reasoned, cannot suffice because, as noted earlier, the deepest doubts stem from uncertainties about the situation both in Southeast Asia and within the United States, and the will of the American people.

The benefits of the Nixon Doctrine are varied, and in some cases, still difficult to measure or guarantee. The greatest potential gain is the creation of a policy viable for the years ahead, suitably adjusted to the realities of the world *and* those at home. Clearly, the new policy aims at reducing the unilateral obligations previously borne by the American people. It also provides increased flexibility for the United States. It is the only nation at this point able to interact seriously with all three of the other major states of East Asia,

Japan, the Soviet Union, and China. Indeed, whether Americans like it or not, the United States is now the vital apex of two critical triangular relations: the Soviet-American-Chinese triangle, involving as it does a full range of political and military concerns centering upon the issues of peaceful coexistence and weapons control; and the Japanese-American-West European triangle, which must wrestle with the problems of cooperation and competition implicit in a a dynamic, intense economic relationship; the appropriate balance of responsibilities for security in a still dangerous world, and the problems as well as the benefits of extensive cultural interaction among advanced societies.

Japan and the Asian Scene

Japan, in evaluating her situation in Asia and in the world, must weigh the various alternatives against the complex and fluid positions of the three large states to which we have just referred, although she cannot dismiss relations with the rest of Asia as insignificant. Historically, Japan faced one major decision similar to that confronting another island society, Great Britain. Should her primary energies be directed toward interaction with the neighboring continent, or aloofness from it? To this issue in modern times has been coupled another: should the nation's basic international ties be regional, or more broadly international in character?

In the historic past, Japan generally sought to preserve her integrity by minimal involvement with the Asian continent, although periodic forays onto the Korean peninsula took place, and strong infusions of Chinese culture were received. Nonetheless, isolation was an established policy when Japanese society was forcibly opened by the West in the mid-nineteenth century. In later decades, Japan was to support her policies in Asia through alliances outside Asia, a highly effective policy until the massive expansion of the 1930s which ended in total defeat.

After World War II, Japan came under American tutelage, with both domestic and foreign policies being shaped accordingly. From an unequal but highly beneficial relationship with the United States, Japan achieved a minimal-risk, maximal-gain foreign policy. That policy had two central elements. First, an intense preoccupation with economic growth developed with a vision of the world cast almost wholly in economic terms — markets, sources of raw materials, opportunities for investment. For both economic and political reasons, moreover, the crucial economic interaction became that with the advanced Western world in general, and the United States in particular. Second, there ensued only the most minimal cultivation of political authority or military power on the international scene. Japan not only depended extensively upon the United States to provide it with security, spending less than one percent of its GNP on defense, but it also undertook very few ventures in political initiative.

The essence of this policy was political identification with an American-centered world, with such independent internationalism as was pursued being expressed through the United Nations. Critics asserted that Japan had no foreign policy, only a program of economic expansion. Even supporters generally accepted the fact that the foreign policy of Japan was extensively dependent upon American initiatives. As one of their prominent spokesmen was to argue, however, did not this policy serve Japanese interests exceedingly well during the era when the United States had the power and the will to maintain an American order in the critical regions of the world? Japan had indeed concentrated upon economic expansion and eschewed the role of "star performer" on the international scene. But what had happened subsequently to such stars as Nasser, Sukarno, and Nkrumah and more important, to their nations?[1]

Times have changed, however, and the burning issue in Japan today is how to cope with those changes. Before turning to the questions that will determine the nature of American-Japanese relations in the years ahead, let us summarize the broader political environment of Asia as it currently exists:

1. A loosely-knit multipolarism is making its appearance on the global scene, with special consequences in Asia. In this region at least, bipolarism no longer represents the essence of the current international order. New, quasi-independent sources of power have emerged and old sources of authority have been challenged or weakened. In particular, the deep fissures that have opened up in Communist ranks, especially the Sino-Soviet cleavage, have served as a catalyst for profound changes in power relations. But important changes have also occurred in the non-Communist world. The dynamic growth of the states of Western Europe and Japan, accompanied by the end of traditional colonialism, has introduced a multitude of new variables into an already complex world. In certain respects, these developments have reduced the capacity of the so-called super-powers to control events, jointly or singly.

At the same time, this is not an age of equidistant multipolarism. It is not a time when international relations are symmetrical and complete. Bilateral relations and alliances, in modified form at least, thus remain supremely important. The international order, moreover, has many lacunae and structural weaknesses. The risks of direct confrontations remain, particularly in Asia where the nation-building process remains unfinished, grave developmental weaknesses plague a number of societies, and there is no agreement upon the status quo.

2. Despite the partial demise of bipolarism, the credibility of Soviet power is at an all-time high in East Asia, the Russians having demonstrated both their strength and their resolve on a wide variety of fronts. With success, however, has come new responsibilities, *and* new problems. At present, Soviet policy is concentrated strongly upon the containment of China.

3. The uncertainties surrounding China and her future role in Asia relate at least as much to questions of internal developments as to decisions on foreign policy. A new leadership in Peking could conceivably make some dramatic changes in policies at home and abroad. A succession crisis after Mao, moreover, might adversely affect China's unity and strength. At present, however, Peking is determined to thwart Russian containment by resistance rather than accommodation; to enter into dialogue with the United States and thereby achieve increased flexibility while at the same time seeking to weaken the non-Communist alliance structure in Asia; and to contain Japan politically and militarily, if not economically. China has also put the world on notice that it intends to be a nuclear power, and play a special role in Asia.

4. The credibility of the United States is currently in doubt in many quarters in Asia, causing fierce debates and sharp policy cleavages among America's allies, neutrals, and its erstwhile opponents. The transition from an American-centered East Asia toward a multipolar Asia has proven to be a traumatic experience for many Asian states and leaders, with the final outcome very unclear at this point.

This is an age of striking paradoxes. No one questions, for example, the current capacities of American military power or even the essential strength of the American economy. The uncertainties revolve around American will and the outcome of the ongoing American domestic revolution, a revolution that has been underway for decades and now appears to be reaching a climax. Rarely in history has there been such an intimate connection between domestic and international politics.

Meanwhile, however, despite all of the uncertainties concerning its future role, the United States remains the only truly omnipresent element in the East Asian scene today, possessing a flexibility with respect to all other principal actors available to none of them. Participating in several vital bilateral relations, and standing at the apex of the two critical triangular groups in the contemporary world, the United States remains a society capable of determining by its actions or inactions the fate of many peoples, however much Americans might wish to cast off that burden.

5. Japan faces the 1970s as an economic giant and a political-military dwarf. The task of how, or whether to balance economic, political and military inputs in fashioning a foreign policy for the future will preoccupy the Japanese — both leaders and citizens — during the crucial years immediately ahead. Japan must now define her national requirements and interests, and shape a policy to meet these in an age when "multipolarity" is of increasing significance in the world at large and "autonomous diplomacy" is the popular slogan of the hour at home.

THE ECONOMIC FACTORS IN AMERICAN-JAPANESE RELATIONS

Let us examine first the economic aspects of American-Japanese relations. It is these aspects that have provided much of the substance of our mutual ties, and also some of the most serious problems of the immediate past.

In the course of presenting its recommendations concerning Japanese trade and industry policies for the 1970s, the Council on Industrial Structure of Japan captured the essence of Japanese economic achievement since 1945 in the following passage: "We have energetically climbed a narrow and steep slope with our eyes intently set on the distant clouds over the mountain. Given such an effort, Japan's economy now stands on the summit of the mountain and views the wide world below."[2]

That lyrical passage is scarcely an exaggeration. With slightly over 100 million people, Japan now has a Gross National Product of $200 billion [$250 billion since yen revaluation], a figure exceeding the combined GNP of all other Asian nations — which have a population eighteen times that of Japan.[3] During the 1960s the growth rate of the Japanese economy averaged 11.3 percent per annum in real terms, the fastest rate of growth among industrial nations. By 1968, Japan had achieved the third highest GNP in the world, surpassed only by the United States and the Soviet Union.

Under the impetus of this extraordinary growth, the structure of the Japanese economy has steadily changed. By 1970, agriculture, forestry and fisheries accounted for only 9 percent of the net domestic product, although farmers constituted approximately 25 percent of the population. (This latter figure represented a steady decline during recent years.) By 1971, moreover, among farm households, only 15.2 percent were wholly dependent upon farm income (compared to 34.3 percent in 1960), whereas 55 percent were primarily dependent upon nonagricultural income (compared to 32.1 percent in 1960). Manufacturing accounted for 31 percent of the net domestic product in 1970, and services for 44 percent. Clearly, Japan now constitutes the prototype of an advance industrial society.

It is interesting to compare the industrial structure of Japan with that of the United States as the 1970s opened:[4]

Percentage of Total Industrial Production

	Japan	United States
Textiles	8.6	7.3
Chemicals	8.9	17.2
Iron and Steel	7.3	5.1
Nonelectrical Machinery	14.7	10.8
Electrical Machinery	15.2	8.4
Transport Machinery	11.2	11.8
Other	34.1	39.4

Within the industrial structures of these two advanced states the major differences, it will be noted, pertain to chemicals and machinery, especially electrical machinery. The percentage of U.S. chemical production within the industrial sector is nearly twice that of Japan, whereas the reverse is true with respect to electrical machinery. In broad terms, however, the structures are similar, indicative of the high level of competition, hence of friction, in recent years.

The Sources of Japanese Growth

How was rapid Japanese growth achieved? Basically, Japan is a supreme example of the fact that if a society is highly acculturated to economic modernization, physical destruction can be overcome. At the close of World War II, the odds against success admittedly seemed formidable. Amidst the rubble of wartime devastation a huge population existed, much of it superfluous given the productive capacities of the time. Resources at home were negligible, but there was no foreign exchange with which to acquire the needed imports. Morale among the people was low, and confidence in the national leadership minimal.

The scene was discouraging indeed, and the mood among all analysts, Japanese and American, deeply pessimistic. It is startling to read the predictions about Japan's future that emanated from the immediate postwar years, and even lingered on into the 1950s. The emphasis was almost exclusively upon the hopelessness of creating an economy that could sustain growth and underwrite prosperity.

Why were all the experts wrong? First, the contributions of the United States were major ones, now frequently forgotten. After taking a *laissez faire* attitude toward Japanese economic problems initially ("They are responsible for the disaster — let *them* solve their difficulties"), two crucial facts came to be appreciated. There could be no meaningful movement toward democracy on the part of a starving people. Moreover, in the final analysis the United States would have to support an impoverished Japan, given the character of our obligations there, adding to the already heavy burdens of the American citizen. Thus, after a brief, spectacular "punishment and reform" era, the American Occupation began to work closely with Japanese officials in fashioning a program for economic stabilization, then rehabilitation and recovery. The precise amount of American funds going into this program, directly and indirectly, will never be known, but they can be estimated at between four and six billion dollars. The Korean War, coming as it did at a critical point, after stabilization had been accomplished, provided a major stimulus, with American purchases from the Japanese market rising sharply.

Yet no amount of American assistance would have sufficed had the recipient not been prepared for its effective use. At this point, that unique combination of cultural, organizational, and behavioral patterns marking modern Japanese society was committed to the central task of economic growth. A modified traditionalism provided the necessary elements of authority, discipline, and sacrifice, forwarding a work ethic that was exceeded in no contemporary society.

The Japanese organizational genius, having its social foundations in the small group and its political expression in oligarchy, had long demonstrated those qualities of stability and flexibility so essential to the process of economic development. Small-group units had proven capable of being aggregated into large-scale industrial operations, moreover, without losing the elements of intimacy, commitment, and cohesion that had been their strength.

At the very center of the Japanese industrial revolution was a very special blend of centralized governmental planning, supervision, and guidance on the one hand, and a vigorous, competitive private enterprise system on the other. Japan had been experimenting with economic growth for nearly one hundred years, and from the Meiji era onward, modernization had been developed and refined on these foundations.

Thus, after the initial support of the Occupation had been supplied, it was possible for the indigenous system to reassert itself. In the broadest sense, the task of that system, as viewed from within, was not merely to restore the Japanese economy but to keep it continuously at the highest level of efficiency by preventing too extensive competition on the one hand, or a series of monopolies on the other. Unrestrained competition would encourage a waste of resources and other inefficiencies which Japan could not afford; moreover, industry had to be able to benefit from the economies of scale. Yet monopolies would mean fewer incentives for innovation, a creeping conservatism at all levels that would take the dynamism out of the economy.[5] The Japanese government, through such crucial branches as the Ministry of Finance and the Ministry of International Trade and Industry (MITI), has dedicated itself to meeting these problems during the past two decades with substantial support from the private sector.

In surveying the postwar record, one can point to a number of critical decisions that emerged from the close interaction between Japanese government and industry. One of the most basic, of course, was the decision to focus upon economic objectives internationally rather than upon political or military ones. The almost exclusive concentration upon economic concerns in the foreign arena, and particularly, upon outlets for Japanese goods and sources for raw materials, earned the Japanese the label, "economic animal," a term not infrequently used in Japan itself. Both political and military ties extraneous to economic concerns were generally avoided. This was the essence of the minimal-risk, maximal-gain foreign policy that became Japan's hallmark during the 1950s.

Of nearly equal importance was the early, critical decision to encourage an emphasis upon capital- and technology-intensive industries, thus placing Japan, a decade or so later, in the forefront of the world's producers of iron and steel, oil refining, petrochemicals, machine production including industrial machinery, automobiles, aircraft, and all types of electronic equipment. As they emerged, moreover, these industries were given strong protection from foreign competition through various restrictions upon imports. At the same time, MITI and other governmental agencies made special efforts to acquire capital for industrial expansion through government-sponsored loans. Road blocks were placed in front of foreign capital investment, thereby keeping national control of the economy in Japanese hands at every level.

Restrictions upon foreign capital, however, did not prevent a dynamic program of investment. In Japan, the ratio of investment to GNP has been approximately 38-39 percent in recent years, double the rate in the United States. The ratio of private capital investment has also been very high. This was made possible by the exceedingly high propensity to save. The ratio of savings to disposable income has been between 20-22 percent in recent years, one of the highest such ratios in the world.

Another significant advantage has been a well-educated, strongly motivated labor force. The educational level of the modern Japanese worker is one of the highest in the world. This fact has enabled Japan to easily absorb the latest technological advances in industry. As a consequence, labor productivity has risen sharply for more than two decades, keeping ahead of wage and salary increases. And while those increases have been substantial as of 1970, the wage level in Japan was only 30 percent of that in the United States.

Industrial relations, meanwhile, built upon a strongly paternalist tradition, have been far more stable than in most other countries operating under comparable systems and at similar stages of development. Guaranteed lifetime employment for regular workers, extensive seniority benefits, an elaborate bonus system, and single-enterprise unionism have tended to reduce the costs and disruptions of labor disputes.

Trade And The Growing Crisis

Taken together, the above factors constitute the central reasons for the strong competitive position that Japan has established and held in the international market in recent years.[6] In the decade of the 1960s, when world trade was increasing at an average annual rate of 9.3 percent, Japan's exports were rising at an average annual rate of 16.9 percent, her imports at 15 percent. In the last four years, moreover, a true "great leap forward" occurred, with exports gaining at a rate of more than 20 percent per annum, reaching a high point of a 24.5 percent increase in 1971 over 1970. Of equal importance, they were heavily concentrated in a few sectors of the market. Since 1965, the balance of trade has been favorable to Japan, and by 1970 foreign exchange reserves were rapidly mounting. At the end of 1971, they exceeded $15.2 billion.

Since the American market constituted a primary Japanese target, the ingredients of a crisis were at hand. In 1970, when Japanese exports totalled nearly $19 billion, approximately 30 percent went to the United States. Of the exports to the United States 72 percent were the products of heavy and chemical industries; 24 percent the products of light industries; and only 4 percent raw materials. Japanese products accounted for 14.7 percent of all American imports. In the same year, Japanese imports totalled $15 billion, and again, approximately 30 percent came from the United States. American exports to Japan were composed largely of raw materials (58 percent), secondarily of machinery (25 percent), and chemical products (7 percent). These trends were accentuated in 1971 when Japanese exports to the United States reached $7.5 billion, increasing 26.5 percent in a single year, while imports from the United States totalled slightly less than $5 billion, a decline of 10.5 percent compared to 1970. Thus, for the United States, the 1971 bilateral trade deficit stood at more than $2.5 billion.[7]

The fact that total trade between Japan and the United States reached $12.5 billion in 1971 testifies to the extraordinary importance of our bilateral economic relations today. That importance is underlined, moreover, by noting GNP trends. In 1970, as noted earlier, Japanese GNP reached nearly $200 billion, with U.S. GNP standing at $975 billion; the combination of the two represented close to 40 percent of the world's total GNP for that year.

Yet these same figures suggest the serious issues that have emerged on the economic front. The storm clouds were on the horizon at least seven years ago. The United States, long the champion of economic liberalism and undisputed leader of the "Free World" economy, found itself in progressive difficulties. A low growth rate, unemployment, rising per unit production costs, inflation — the combination which has come to be known as "stagflation" — afflicted the American economy, making it sluggish at home and increasingly noncompetititive abroad. As confidence in the U.S. economy weakened, the American dollar recurrently fell into trouble, and the international monetary system itself went through periodic crises. An intensifying European regionalism and unrestrained Japanese growth exacerbated the problems.

From the beginning of the critical period, moreover, economic issues between Japan and the United States had sharp political connotations, especially in America. U.S. exports to Japan in the main were noncompetitive, being largely composed of raw materials and foodstuffs. Japanese exports to the United States, however, were highly competitive, centering first upon textiles, then moving to such sensitive fields as iron and steel, electronic equipment, and automobiles.

Against this background, let us examine the trade issue as it has affected our mutual relations, and the alternatives that lie ahead. The troubled era between Washington and Tokyo was inaugurated by the textile crisis. Textiles, once accounting for 50 percent of Japan's total exports in the prewar era, had declined sharply in relative importance after 1945, but even in 1970 they accounted for 15 percent of Japanese exports, not a negligible amount. Despite the establishment of "voluntary quotas," these exports had long plagued the American textile industry, an ailing industry but one with continuing political strength, especially in the south. Both of the American presidential candidates of 1968 had pledged additional remedial action, if elected.

Reportedly, Prime Minister Sato promised to settle the textile issue satisfactorily at the time of the Nixon-Sato

Conference in November 1969. The Japanese textile industry, however, proved to be exceedingly tough, and the issue became deeply involved in the politics of both Japan and the United States. Subsequent events, indeed, threatened to create an unbridgeable cleavage between Nixon and Sato, with the President furious over developments. Negotiations were finally broken off on June 23, 1970, just one day after the automatic extension of the Mutual Security Treaty.

For many reasons, the textile issue was deeply regretable. Yet it was also illustrative of some of the most stubborn problems confronting American-Japanese economic relations. Actually, in 1970 Japanese textiles constituted only 1.3 percent of the total U.S. textile sales, but they were heavily concentrated in certain segments of the market. Nor were Japanese textiles by any means the only foreign textiles offering serious competition to American producers. Textiles from such places as South Korea, Taiwan, and Hong Kong were coming into the American market too. (At home, Japanese producers were also beginning to feel the effects of foreign textile imports.)

Despite its political vitality in some regions, moreover, the American textile industry faces a doubtful future. This is one of those industries where governmental adjustment assistance might be warranted, to help phase out a sick industry while encouraging the creation of new technologies and industries, thereby moving the United States to ever higher industrial levels. If the primary effort of advanced nations goes into protecting declining industries, the costs will be extensive and the results dubious.

In the case of textiles, a temporary solution was reached after three years of bickering when on January 3, 1972, an official agreement governing imports was concluded. But meanwhile, industries far more vital to the American economy had felt themselves under siege in the Japanese export blitz so rapidly mounted after 1966. In 1970, for example, Japanese crude steel output reached 93 million tons, a 13.6 percent increase over the previous year. Japan had now become the top iron-steel exporter in the world, and of its 18 million metric ton exports, 36.5 percent were sent to North America in that year. In this field as in a number of others, a voluntary quota system has been established to slow down the invasion. In 1969, a three-year agreement limiting Japanese steel exports in quantitative growth to 5 percent per annum had been reached, an agreement now scheduled to be renewed for an additional three years, with the limit reduced to 2.5 percent.

In the automobile industry, where Japan has had the highest growth rate in the world in recent years, exports increased sharply, with 50 percent coming to the United States. The American electrical appliance market was also challenged by Japanese competition, with heavy inroads beginning in 1968-1969. Color television sets from Japan flooded the market, and American producers protested strongly against the Japanese dual price system, asserting that the Japanese were selling a number of products abroad considerably under their domestic prices, thereby engaging in "dumping."

The American business community's complaints might be summarized as follows: The Japanese government, contrary to its American counterpart, operates in close collusion with Japanese business. Official support is given to the creation of cartels, for example, when big foreign markets are at stake. Extensive, governmentally funded studies are undertaken of the international market situation, enabling Japanese traders to determine the most vulnerable markets. Low interest loans are then made available from the government-dominated banking system, with some 80 percent of the financing coming from this source. Japan also has the lowest corporate taxes in the industrial world.

Armed with these advantages, the Japanese entrepreneurs are able to conduct blitzkrieg operations against foreign markets, first attacking one sector and, when that has been conquered, moving against another. Thus, such American industries as textiles and electronics have suffered heavily in a relatively short period of time. Meanwhile, through "administrative guidance," MITI and other agencies of the Japanese government have allegedly exercised a generally protectionist role despite the removal of formal restraints on foreign sales and investments. MITI may "advise" local firms to buy domestic products, to expand or restrict production, or to obtain funds without recourse to foreign involvements. Exchange controls have been complete in Japan, with no convertible currency system; hence the yen has not been free, and the real competitive position of Japan has not been fully tested.

Needless to say, this analysis is not fully accepted by the Japanese, nor by some other observers. Alternate views might be summarized as follows: The thesis of a "Japan Incorporated" has been greatly exaggerated. Governmental assistance to the private sector of the economy is no greater than that provided by certain countries of Western Europe. Nor is Japanese business monolithic. Competition is fierce, ruling out most types of coordination or collusion in overseas marketing. Indeed, the cutthroat competition *within* the Japanese economy may represent the heart of the problem, since survival depends upon the use of all available sales and marketing techniques, and the acceptance of low profit and margin. Moreover, while protectionism was admittedly substantial until 1968, since that time, it is asserted, major steps have been taken to make Japan one of the least restrictive nations in the industrial world.

Japanese competitiveness, it is argued, despite some unfair practices, derives in major part from superior salesmanship, servicing arrangements, credits, and similar evidences of hard work. The most fundamental problems facing the American economy are due to internal weaknesses, some of which contribute to its increasing lack of competitiveness in world markets. It is thus unfair to make Japan a scapegoat for American deficiencies — including a considerable loss of the work ethic.

As usual, the truth in these matters is complex and probably best served by some combination of these arguments. The relations between government and business differ considerably in the American and Japanese systems and unquestionably give Japanese business some significant advantages in international competition. Moreover, the evidence is overwhelming that in the past unrestrained Japanese export expansion, conducted with lightening-like speed and often heavily concentrated in a few sectors, has made political repercussions inevitable.[8] Indeed, Japan has found the American market ideal because it is a sophisticated market, capable of absorbing products in large quantities, hence underwriting the type of sales and service campaign which the Japanese are now capable of sustaining.

Nor are the charges of "dumping" without foundation in certain cases. Japanese pricing policies, costs, and profits are all closely guarded secrets, but there is reason to question certain Japanese business practices, both with respect to the United States and elsewhere. On the other hand, few would deny that the American economy has been in serious trouble during recent years, and the issue of whether the United States can be competitive remains a crucial, yet unanswered, question, with implications that go far beyond our bilateral relations with Japan. The Japanese claim, moreover, that their liberalization has proceeded very rapidly since 1968 is correct, and the charge that current American trends seem to be in the opposite direction also has validity.

In the late 1960s, pressures mounted within the United States for protectionist policies going far beyond the earlier insistence upon a few voluntary quotas. Thus, in 1970 a bill passed the House of Representatives authorizing the establishment of quotas on any foreign product that obtained as much as 15 percent of the U.S. market — a measure clearly aimed at Japan. The bill died in the Senate, but various other measures have been proposed, and protectionist sentiment remains high.

Some fairly dramatic developments occurred during 1971-1972, however. From the beginning of 1971, Japan pushed liberalization with great vigor. The items subject to import restrictions were reduced from 80 to 34 by April 1, 1972, involving 17 industrial items. At the same time, as of February 1, 1972, the Japanese government moved to abolish the automatic import quota (AIQ) system which had been strongly criticized as a nontariff barrier, leaving only 11 items on the AIQ list.

At the San Clemente Meeting of January 6-7, 1972, moreover, President Nixon and Prime Minister Sato agreed that the two countries should push the so-called Japan-round tariff cuts proposed by the Japanese side relating to long-term commerce and that a committee of experts should be established to improve the application of U.S. anti-dumping laws. This was followed one month later by the Agreement of February 10, reached between William Eberle, the President's special trade negotiator, and Ambassador Ushiba. That agreement pledged the commencement of comprehensive, multilateral negotiations within the framework of the General Agreement on Tariffs and Trade (GATT), beginning in 1973. Prior to that time, a one-year truce on U.S.-Japan trade problems would be maintained. Meanwhile, tariff reductions covering some 238 items, both agricultural and industrial products, were initiated.

The advanced industrial world now faces an uncomfortable, possibly grave situation. The signs of protectionism are by no means confined to the United States. They are also strongly apparent within the European Economic Community (EEC). Indeed, it is clear that two powerful contradictory trends are now running in the world. As the first major steps toward regionalism and internationalism are being taken in the economic sphere, protectionist reactions of varying intensity are emerging, some of them reflective of the frustrations involved in these efforts, others products of the regionalist policies themselves. The events of the next several years may well determine which basic set of trends will predominate.

The Kennedy round of talks, which lasted for five years, resulted in major steps being taken toward more open trade, with tariff reductions, primarily on industrial goods, averaging 30 percent. The aim in the new international round of talks is to involve nearly 100 countries, and to encompass not merely tariff reductions, but also the removal of nontariff barriers and the relaxation of agricultural import restrictions. Thus, it will represent one of the most ambitious undertakings in the history of international relations. And the central actors will be the United States, Japan, and the nations of the European Economic Community.

Since many complex problems remain to be resolved — problems reaching deeply into the political as well as the economic realm — the discussions are likely to extend over a very considerable period of time and to involve negotiations at many levels. Already, within each of the nations principally involved, serious internal divisions have made themselves manifest. In Japan, for example, the Ministry of Agriculture and Forestry, reflecting agrarian interests, strongly opposed the initiation of a new round at this time. In Europe, France has generally played a negative role. The ultimate outcome, crucial to U.S.-Japan relations as well as to Japan-U.S.-EEC triangular relations, cannot be predicted at this time, but we may stand on the threshhold of a promising new era in the economic relations of all societies.

Economic Trends in The United States and Japan

Meanwhile, the "Nixon shock" of August 15, 1971, symbolized the troubled nature of the era through which we have just been passing. The measures announced on August 15 were undertaken in an effort to challenge the highly adverse U.S. balance of payments, inflation, and unemployment, and to force the hitherto reluctant nations of West Europe and Japan to take measures that would relieve pressure upon the United States. One immediate effort was to force a revaluation of certain foreign currencies, notably the yen, and in effect, to look toward a new international monetary system. After a series of events including intensive bilateral and multilateral negotiations, the Smithsonian Agreement on currency adjustment was reached among nine nations, including Japan, on December 18, 1971. The yen was revalued upward 16.88 percent, a figure considerably higher than had been desired by the Japanese business community.

Taken together, the recent changes together with the actions now contemplated for the future, have gone far to reduce the sense of immediate crisis in our bilateral economic relations. It would be entirely premature, however, to imply that the crisis is at an end or that fundamental solutions are in sight. It is even too early to measure with any precision the impact of the measures which have already been taken. Some observers believe that it will take up to five years for a satisfactory economic relationship between the United States and Japan to be worked out, even assuming optimal developments. In exploring the longer range prospects for our mutual economic relations, therefore, we are confronted with a number of highly uncertain factors. Before turning directly to the future, however, let us look at some of the weaknesses of the Japanese economy, having earlier examined its strengths. It is imperative to keep such a balance sheet in mind when contemplating future trends.

As in most rapidly developing or highly industrialized societies, Japan faces the constant problem of inflation. During the decade of the 1960s, consumer prices rose on an average of 5 percent per annum. In 1970, the rise was 7.7 percent, and in 1971 nearly 6 percent. One element contributing to this development has been wage increases. Japanese wages have risen significantly in the past decade. For example, they went up on an average of 18 percent in 1970 — while productivity was rising 14 percent. By that year, Japanese wages had reached an average of 94 cents an hour, above the average for Italy and France, but less than one-third of the average American wage.

However, a domestic labor shortage will increasingly affect Japan during the 1970s, and certain projections indicate that by the end of that decade Japanese labor costs will amount to 80 percent of those of the United States. For these reasons, and also to reduce the very serious problems of pollution, and to have ready access to raw materials, Japanese industry is likely to seek production sites in a number of the developing societies outside Japan in the course of the coming decade. This trend, indeed, is already underway.

As has been emphasized, the current theme in Japanese

political circles is the necessity of some reorientation of priorities from economic growth toward social services. Currently, much attention is being given to plans to increase expenditures for housing, roads, recreational facilities, and a wide range of welfare programs. With such problems as pollution extremely acute, moreover, industrial costs might be expected to rise in the course of taking remedial actions. It is quite possible, of course, that the level of Japanese tolerance on some problems (pollution, for example) will remain significantly higher than that of the United States.

Projections for 1980

How do the Japanese themselves see the coming decade in economic terms? Official projections signal clearly that it will not be easy to avoid substantial problems in U.S.-Japanese economic relations. If the recommendations of several Japanese study groups are accepted, the industrial composition of Japan will shift toward information-intensive type industries, with a heavy emphasis upon electronics, aircraft, new synthetic chemicals, sophisticated assembly industries, and fashion industries including clothing, furniture, and household appliances. In part, this would represent an effort to make Japanese industry less dependent upon extensive labor and large quantities of raw materials. But it also foreshadows greater, rather than less, competition with the United States, since it is in many of these fields that American preeminence exists.

Despite the pledge to invest much more heavily in social services and improvements in the quality of Japanese life, moreover, current projections call for a growth rate averaging 8 percent per annum during the 1970s, only slightly less than the 10-11 percent achieved in the previous decade, and a phenomenally high rate of growth, especially for an advanced society. It is possible, of course, that the goal will not be reached. Real growth in 1971 was 5.6 percent, considerably below this goal! Based on that rate, however, total Japanese GNP would reach $957 billion by 1980, not far below the U.S. figure of $1,065 billion for 1971.

To sustain such a growth rate, moreover, Japan is counting heavily upon a steady expansion of her foreign trade, and — despite the new emphasis within her industrial structure — upon greatly increased quantities of raw materials and energy sources. By 1975, raw materials and energy sources, which accounted for slightly over 10 percent of all Japanese imports in 1966, are scheduled to grow to nearly 21 percent, and by 1980, the projected figure is 30 percent. For example, the Japanese demand for petroleum is expected to increase 4.6-fold, that for aluminum over 3-fold, and for copper, 2.6-fold. The drive to obtain uranium also promises to be intense, as Japan seeks to increase her nuclear power capacities. Heightened competition among the world's more advanced industrial states for raw materials and energy sources thus seems inevitable, and it will surely involve the two leaders; the United States and Japan.

Meanwhile, Japan hopes to expand her share of the total world export trade from 6.2 percent in 1970 to 10.8 percent in 1980 (with world trade expected to increase on an average of 10.6 percent per annum). The U.S. share of world export trade in 1970 was 14.2 percent; that of West Germany was 12.2 percent. In value, total Japanese import trade would go from $15 billion in 1970 to $75.5 billion in 1980, while exports rose from $19 billion to $92.2 billion during the same period. Japan assumes that exports of labor-intensive products will decline from 28 percent of her total export trade in 1970 to 15 percent in 1980, with compensation through major gains in the technology- or capital-intensive products noted earlier.

What is the anticipation with respect to the structure of this trade? Present projections suggest only modest changes. According to current planning, 32.4 percent of Japanese exports and 31.4 percent of imports will be with North America, as opposed to 34.1 percent and 34.5 percent respectively in 1970. Thus, Japan expects to continue its intensive economic relations with the United States. Exports to West Europe in 1980, as opposed to 15.1 percent in 1970, are expected to represent 19.2 percent of Japanese exports in 1980, with imports from this region totalling 15.5 percent (compared to 10.9 percent in 1970). Little change is anticipated also in trade with Australia, New Zealand, and South Africa; Japanese exports being projected in 1980 at 5.6 percent, compared to 5.5 percent in 1970, and imports at 9.5 percent as compared to 10.4 percent in 1970.

Thus, Japan expects that 57.2 percent of its exports will go to the United States, West Europe, and the ANS nations in 1980, with 56.4 percent of its imports coming from those nations. These figures illustrate that throughout the coming decade, economic relations with the advanced nations, and particularly with the United States and West Europe, will remain as vital as they have in the past.

According to 1980 projections, one-third of Japan's export-import trade will be with the developing nations, a continuance of the present rate. With the Communist states some gains are anticipated. Export trade, totalling 5.4 percent in 1970 with these states, is predicted to rise to 8.6 percent in 1980; imports, which were at 4.9 percent in 1970, are forecast at 9.7 percent in 1980.

Trade and the Major Communist States

Since trade with the Communist states, and particularly with the Soviet Union and the Chinese People's Republic, has important political as well as economic implications, a more thorough examination of current trends and future prospects is warranted. In 1971, trade between Japan and China totalled about $900 million, nearly 90 percent of it through "friendly firms." This development has a lengthy and somewhat checkered history. In August 1960, after trade had been virtually suspended for two years because of an earlier incident, Chou En-lai proposed that until diplomatic relations between the two nations were normalized, trade be conducted through Japanese companies pledged to friendliness with China. In November 1962, a new development took place. Liao Cheng-chih and Takasaki Tatsunosuke exchanged a memorandum establishing certain principles for quasi-official trade between the two countries. This was the beginning of the so-called L-T trade, later (1968) replaced by "memorandum trade," which is annually renewed.

The Chinese People's Republic has consistently sought to tie trade and politics together. In recent years, all would-be Japanese traders must adhere to the "four principles," including the agreement that there is only one China and that Taiwan is a part of China.[9] Increasingly, the declarations jointly issued after trade negotiations have represented concessions to Peking's views, including trenchant attacks upon "Japanese militarism" and the policies of the Japanese government. Privately, some of the Japanese participants in these exercises dismiss the joint statements as meaningless, a necessary formality in the category of the earlier reading from Mao's collected works enforced upon Japanese business representatives. Gradually, however, the Japanese government has been put under greater pressure from a portion of the business community to accept Chinese conditons for the normalization of political relations.

Certainly, interest in China trade has not diminished. At the 1971 Canton Trade Fair of October 15, no less than 2300 representatives of 1500 Japanese firms were present, including men from both large and small enterprises. But is China destined to be a major element in Japan's economic future? MITI projectons currently provide a negative answer. Under optimum conditions, MITI estimates that Japan-China trade will reach approximately $3.2 billion by 1980 (from $810 million in 1970). This would represent no more than 2 percent of total Japanese trade as projected at that point. MITI assumes that credits would be provided by Japan, and that Japanese exports would consist primarily of iron and steel, machinery, ships, trucks, and similar items, while Chinese imports would be composed essentially of raw materials. Their estimates are predicated upon the assumption of an average Chinese economic growth rate of 8-9 percent, with the total volume of Chinese foreign trade going from $4.2 billion in 1970 to $12 billion in 1980, and Japan garnering slightly over 25 percent of this trade.

Under these conditions, Japanese-Chinese trade would be much more important to Peking than to Tokyo. The trade pattern, moreover, would be the usual one between an advanced and a developing economy: China would import the products necessary to her developmental goals, and export the raw materials available to acquire foreign exchange, with dependence upon trade growing. If Japan expects to obtain as much as one-quarter of the China market, however, political normalization would probably be required, and the conclusion of a commercial treaty and trade agreement between the two governments would be essential.

Prospects for Soviet trade appear more promising, at least in the near future. On September 22, 1971, a new long-term Japanese-Soviet trade agreement was signed in Tokyo calling for two-way transactions amounting to $5.2 billion during the five year period between 1971 and 1975, a 79 percent increase over the previous five years ($3.3 billion). The new agreement calls for a greater diversification of trade as well as increases in volume, with the Japan-Soviet Economic Committee in charge of operations.

Japan first concluded a Treaty of Commerce and Navigation with the Soviet Union in 1957. This has become the basis for subsequent five-year agreements. Japan-Soviet trade rose from $40 million in 1958 to $822 million in 1970, topping China trade for that year, and accounting for 3 percent of Russian trade with non-Communist countries. The present agreement looks toward an annual increase of 12.7 percent in trade during the 1971-1975 period, and is based essentially upon an exchange of Russian timber, oil, coal, iron ore for Japanese machinery, iron and steel products, textiles, and chemical products.

A more dramatic possibility involves the development of Siberia. As is well known, Japan and the Soviet Union have been recently engaged in serious negotiations concerning the possibility of joint operations in Siberia, and some projects have already been approved; a forestry development project and a harbor construction project at Wrangell, a site facing the Sea of Japan. The most ambitious proposal, however, involves the Tyumen Oil Fields. The Russians have proposed that Japan invest approximately $1 billion to aid in the construction of additional pipelines, enabling the flow of gas and oil deposits from the rich Siberian fields to the Pacific Ocean. In exchange, Japan would get up to 8 or 9 percent of her required oil imports.[10]

A Japanese mission is now exploring the economic feasibility of this ambitious project, while the Japanese government contemplates its political implications. Questions relating to financing, the precise amount of oil reserves, and the nature of supply guarantees remain to be answered to the satisfaction of the Japanese. There are also highly important strategic and political matters to be considered. To what extent would this project, when completed, enable the Soviet Union to develop a major naval presence in Northeast Asia, and what would be the strategic implications of that presence? Would this development, and the existence of a pipeline running close to the Sino-Soviet border at points create new tension between Russia and China, and more importantly from the Japanese viewpoint, would a joint project of this nature with the Soviet Union inhibit normalization of Sino-Japanese relations? Or can it be used as a threat or a bargaining point in seeking to moderate current Chinese demands upon Tokyo? All of these questons are at once important and difficult to answer. The "Siberian issue" provides an excellent case study in the close interrelation between economic and political-strategic policies. It may indicate also the extent to which economic power can provide political leverage, or serve as an alternate to military-political power in the preservation of national interests.

Japanese Goals and Their Impact Upon U.S.-Japan Relations

We are now in a position to survey the main course upon which the Japanese economy is launched, and the implications of this course for American-Japanese relations during the 1970s.

1. Despite the conscious efforts to shift from a total preoccupation with economic growth to a greater concern for public welfare — efforts that *will* produce cumulative results of significance in the years immediately ahead — Japan remains committed to a high growth rate throughout the 1970s. Her objectives are to attain an average annual GNP increase of 8 percent. Even if this growth were reduced to 5

or 6 percent, it would still represent one of the most rapid advances within the industrial world.

It is probable that Japan will move ahead of the Soviet Union in productivity before 1980, standing next to the United States as the second most "advanced" industrial society in the world. As we have noted, the United States and Japan together accounted for more than 40 percent of the world's total GNP in 1972, and Japan alone had a production surpassing that of the rest of East Asia combined. We are thus dealing with the interaction between the two most dynamic and powerful societies of the industrial world.

2. The Japanese economy will continue to be much more highly dependent upon foreign trade than comparable economies. Raw materials and energy sources must be obtained abroad, and in ever increasing quantities. Moreover, the dependence of the Japanese economy upon external relations seems certain to increase in other respects as well. The quest for a more abundant labor supply and the desirability of production sites that will not contribute further to metropolitan problems in Japan will encourage the movement of Japanese industries overseas. The multinational corporation potentially has as great significance to Japan as to any Western state, notwithstanding certain cultural obstacles.

3. In her search for markets and sources of raw materials, Japan will overlook no opportunities. The premium will be upon expansion wherever the chance presents itself. In the future as in the past, the developing nations, and particularly those of Southeast Asia, will be important. Latin America and Africa also offer excellent prospects in certain respects. Nor are the new possibilities afforded by the Communist states going to be overlooked.

Nevertheless, Japan's most significant economic relations will continue to be with the "advanced" industrial world, especially with the United States. The condition of American-Japanese economic relations will continue to constitute the most crucial determinant of the Japanese economy, its growth or stagnation, its health or sickness. Moreover, while that relationship will be of great importance to both parties, it will be far more vital to Japan than to the United States.

4. The elements of competiton and potential friction between the United States and Japan in the economic arena will continue to mount in certain areas. In addition to a competition of growing intensity for access to raw materials and energy sources, the structure of the two economies will move in a similar direction — that of higher levels of technology, representing an effort to reduce the extensive dependence upon labor and raw materials, and to take advantage of being on the scientific-technological frontiers of mankind.

5. Japan's substantial economic advantages of recent years over the United States, however, will be reduced in some degree in the course of the decade ahead. Labor costs, as noted earlier, are likely to rise appreciably. Various social welfare and environmental priorities will affect production costs. A rising consumer revolution and a changing culture may also have major impacts upon such aspects of Japanese behavior as the propensity for very high savings. It is even possible that more serious problems lie ahead. Should political instability emerge in Japan, and a trend away from the current mainstream of the Liberal Democratic Party, economic policies and governmental-business relations could both be significantly affected.

6. Such economic issues involving the United States and Japan as monetary policies and trade relations are not merely, perhaps not primarily, bilateral in character. At a minimum, they involve relations among Japan, the United States, and West Europe, with such states of the Pacific Basin

as Australia, Canada, and New Zealand also critically affected.

Policy Alternatives in the Economic Sphere

At this point, it is appropriate to turn to the broad alternatives that confront Japan and the United States in the economic sphere. In the most basic sense, we stand at a crossroads with respect to economic relations among "advanced" nations. On the one hand, many signs indicate a steady, even spectacular growth in economic internationalization — both product and witness of mass production technology, the communications revolution, and a mounting affluence. In the years ahead, it seems likely that all forms of international economic intercourse will advance. At the same time, however, there are many manifestations of an intensified nationalism or a heightened exclusivism not merely among the emerging societies but more particularly among the advanced states. A mood of retreat from the bold international commitments of a few years ago, and a cynicism or indifference to most multinational institutions, is now manifest in both governments and citizens, and not merely in the United States. What has produced the new trend? The frustrations involved in making internationalism operative constitute one factor. Even more important are the complex domestic problems that have accompanied the climactic stages of the industrial revolution, problems that seem to defy solution.

Sometimes, exclusivism takes the form of total withdrawal. Solace is sought in the small group, and primitivism is once again heralded as a virtue. Not merely internationalism but nationalism also is shunned. Sometimes, in contrast, the effort is to concentrate upon regionalism, hence upon economic or political forms going beyond the nation-state —

but with the program being forwarded by the same weapons of exclusivism that were once used to advance the nationalist cause. And in other instances, nationalism — economic or political — attains renewed vigor in an effort to deal with a deepening internal crisis, or with past dependency in mind.

Are we on the verge of entering an age of increasing economic interaction and interdependence; one characterized by the rapid expansion of trade, the growth of foreign capital investment, and the increased sharing of technology? Or will our mutual differences and rivalries so dominate the scene as to render these efforts abortive, and produce a heightened protectionism amounting to economic warfare? The first test is at hand, as renewed multilateral negotiations get underway in 1973.

American-Japanese economic relations must be seen in this broader context. Before examining the steps that might be taken to improve those relations, however, it must be emphasized that there is no panacea — no simple, singular formula whereby the problems of the past will be suddenly eliminated. We are entering a period of intense, prolonged negotiations with allies as well as with opponents, and we can expect most "solutions" to evolve out of the negotiatory process as products of complex compromises and successive stages of development amidst crisis.

The first indispensable step, however, is the reestablishment of a healthy American economy. The United States remains the economic giant of the twentieth century. When it suffers an indisposition, especially if the illness is both serious and prolonged, the economies of all open societies are correspondingly affected. The extraordinary intimacy characterizing American-Japanese economic relations, and the heavy dependence of the Japanese economy upon the United States merely reinforce the urgency of this task.

In the long run, moreover, the health of the American economy must involve a willingness to face up to those basic issues that will determine our international economic position. How do we remain competitive in the world of today and tomorrow? What are the strengths implicit in our culture and stage of development, and how should these be accentuated? How do we slough off outmoded aspects of the economy in the most efficient and expeditious manner, still attentive to social responsibilities?

The answers to these questions may require new institutions as well as new policies. On all sides, it is now admitted that a new labor-management relations system is needed. How do we keep in the forefront of research and development so that the movement to ever higher stages of industrial and agrarian technology enables us to play the role in the international economic order for which we are best suited? Is adjustment assistance advisable so as to aid in the prompt shift from sick and dying industries toward dynamic ones? What policies should be developed with respect to multinational corporations, and to encourage foreign investment, especially Japanese investment, in this country? Are the present anti-trust laws appropriate to this era, and if not, what modifications should be considered?

As was noted earlier, Japan may have reached the peak of advantage vis-à-vis the United States; the gap, however, is likely to remain appreciable for the foreseeable future. The United States must explore methods of revitalizing the industrial component of society, not merely to improve our competitive position with respect to Japan, but with respect to other nations as well, and to bring our economic structure into line with the requirements of the late twentieth century. To this end, a commission might well be established now, with business, labor, consumer, academic, and governmental representatives to undertake a comprehensive study of the central issues, and to make recommendations to the President.

Meanwhile, certain steps can be taken by Japan to alleviate some points of tension, removing at the same time antiquated or economically irrational practices. For example, the Japanese agricultural system is badly in need of a drastic overhauling. Agriculture in Japan is still operated essentially as a cottage industry, under extensive governmental protection, in virtual isolation and with self-sufficiency as a primary objective. Until 1968, the government encouraged an expansion of rice production, subsidizing the farmer extensively. The result was overproduction. Meanwhile, Japanese eating habits were changing, with the consumption of animal proteins and greens rapidly increasing. An effort is now underway to shift the emphasis toward the production of fruit, vegetables, and other specialized items.

In Japan, as in other advanced societies, the political pressures operating on behalf of extensive protectionism in agriculture remain high. As indicated earlier, one-fourth of the Japanese population is still engaged in agriculture, although a majority of this group have important outside sources of income. Two courses of action now seem indicated. The demands for lower consumer prices and inflation controls, together with the requirements for a more balanced international market, support a removal of the protectionist net thrown around Japanese agriculture. Admittedly, this will not be easy, given the heavy dependence of the Japanese conservatives upon the rural voter. At the same time, the bulk of those engaged in that occupation should be shifted into other sectors of the economy and the present agricultural system itself drastically changed, with the premium upon the most advanced techniques and larger production units.

In retrospect, it will probably be said that the year 1972 marked the beginning of Japan's walk down the welfare path. The pace of that walk, understandably, will be very gradual. Only about 14.3 percent of the fiscal 1972 budget was allocated to welfare-related expenditures, approximately one-half the percentage characteristic of U.S. and West European budgets. Nevertheless, the future route has been staked out. A host of services cry out for additional attention: sewage systems, housing, roads, pollution control, and recreational areas are only the most obvious examples. As attention is focused in these directions, the frenetic and concentrated drive on growth alone will be slowed, reducing some of the pressures on the international scene. Some concern has already been expressed that eventually, the problem of stagflation recently witnessed in such countries as the United States and Great Britain may also develop in Japan. This prospect, however, scarcely seems imminent.

Meanwhile, Japanese authorities themselves have come increasingly to realize that orderly exports are necessary if favorable economic and political relations are to be maintained between the United States and Japan. Recently, *Keidanren*, the Federation of Economic Organizations, set up a special committee, the Orderly Marketing Committee, specifically to promote regulated exports by Japanese traders. In principle, Japan accepts that blitzkrieg tactics — the unrestricted saturation of a specific market within a brief period — inevitably provoke resentment and retaliation. Obviously, Japan has a great stake in stopping the rise of protectionism, and promoting freer trade and economic intercourse.

The most appropriate means of obtaining and preserving orderly export policies, however, may require some further experimentation. It is very doubtful that the new committee noted above can be effective by itself. Up to date, a considerable amount of "ad hoc-ery" has been involved. Crisis situations have been allowed to develop, and then, after extensive, often acrimonious discussions, "voluntary quotas" have been established, enabling Japanese exports of given products to the United States to increase only by a fixed percentage.

On occasion, these quotas have been established concurrently with quotas assigned other countries producing the same commodity. Often, however, the quota system has applied to Japan alone. In any case, the present approach to this matter, while having some merits, also has a number of deficiencies. A problem must often reach an explosive stage before attention is focused upon it, thereby insuring a high emotional and political content – and making amicable, rational approaches very difficult.

One possibility at the bilateral level is the creation of a United States-Japan Trade and Investment Commission which would serve as a standing body with mixed membership and an adequate permanent staff. Its chief functions would be to anticipate problems relating to economic intercourse in advance as well as dealing with specific grievances brought to it by any party. In certain instances, it would have the power to act; in other situations, it could advise the respective governments on policies or legislation – unilateral, bilateral, or multilateral.

For these purposes, it might not be necessary to establish a new body. Possibly, the present cabinet-level U.S.-Japan Joint Committee on Trade and Economic Affairs could be so altered in structure and functions as to be used for these purposes. Other bodies now exist (such as the Advisory Council on Japan-United States Relations, a mixed, private business group) that might also be suitable vehicles. The current need, however, is clear. The requirements involved in our bilateral trade and investment demand redefinition, with some appropriate institution specifically addressed to them. As has been indicated, future problems will not pertain primarily to formal tariff restrictions. Nontariff barriers will constitute the central issue, including the complex matter of "administrative guidance." Since such guidance is merely a part of a broader set of institutional and behavioral patterns markedly different from those characterizing the American scene, it will not easily be removed as an issue. Thus, it is critical that some supernational American-Japanese body exist with both governmental and nongovernmental personnel which can acquire data and conduct ongoing discussions on the supremely important question of how we can make our respective economic systems more compatible and supportive in their mutual interaction.

One concrete measure that would greatly improve such interaction would be the expansion of direct Japanese investment in the United States. As of 1970, only 32 Japanese enterprises were operating in the United States, in comparison with the 326 American firms doing business in Japan. Japanese investors have preferred other areas for a number of reasons: cheap labor, markets easy to penetrate, and more generally, confidence in their ability to compete effectively. Japanese entrepreneurs in many cases still harbor an inferiority complex toward American business, notwithstanding their major successes of recent years.

Recently, however, MITI has begun to explore those measures that might stimulate Japanese direct investment in the United States. A Japanese mission is being sent to America to look into possibilities. The application of the investment insurance system to firms commencing activities in the United States is being considered. Also being explored is the question of how the immigration of Japanese workers to the United States can be facilitated, with the staffing of such operations in mind. These activities signal the hope that within five years, significant Japanese investments will aid in improving our trade balance, as well as in tieing our two economies more intimately together.

Despite the importance of pursuing the efforts outlined above on a bilateral basis, the multilateral dimensions of trade, monetary and investment policies are commonly acknowledged. The triangle vital to the economic health and wealth of much of the world at present is that composed of Japan, the United States, and West Europe as we have emphasized. The forthcoming international round of talks on the reduction of tariff rates, the removal of nontariff barriers, and the elimination of agricultural import restrictions (now scheduled to begin in 1973) will be of critical importance. But as indicated earlier, given present trends and the general political mood prevailing, quick and easy progress on most fronts cannot be expected. West Europe, more particularly the EEC, has also supported protectionism in recent years, particularly with respect to agriculture, and has exhibited — perhaps understandably — a great fear of Japan, practicing discrimination against both Japan and the United States on certain fronts.[11] Thus, the outcome of these negotiations may well spell out the nature of the economic system of the advanced world for the next decade and beyond.

Meanwhile, multilateralism of a different type might well be contemplated, not as a substitute but as a supplement. The creation of a Pacific Basin Community as a counterpart or complement to the OECD (Organization for Economic Cooperation and Development) warrants serious consideration. The economic relations among the United States, Japan, Canada, Australia and New Zealand are particularly intimate, closely interrelated, and vitally important. They involve both special problems and mutual interests. The functions of such a group would relate to the full range of issues connected with economic interaction among the member states and to questions connected with economic aid to the late developing countries of the region. A Pacific Basin Economic Cooperation Committee presently exists, but its functions are at best embryonic. Is it not time to make a serious start at economic regionalism among the advanced states of the Pacific-Asian region?

The future of the so-called "North-South" problem is of particular importance both to the prosperity and to the peace of this vast area, and developments at the moment are far from encouraging. While the United States is still the largest contributor to aid and development, the political tides are running against aid in its present forms at least, and only a bold, new program involving multilateral agreements would be likely to reverse these tides. Japanese foreign assistance, meanwhile, has increased, but betrays a number of grave deficiencies. In 1970, Japan's foreign aid amounted to $1.8 billion on a disbursement basis, making it the second largest donor in the world. This constituted nearly 1 percent of Japan's GNP, the international goal for developed countries established by the Development Assistance Committee of the OECD for 1975. The quality of Japanese aid is, however, still poor, and government aid (as opposed to aid from private sources) constitutes only about 25 percent of total Japanese aid. One of the criticisms of the program as presently operating is that it is essentially a scheme to promote Japanese exports rather than a genuine assistance program. This charge is valid. A high percentage of the export credit and aid is tied to purchases of Japanese commodities, representing commercial loans to finance business transactions. In addition, loan terms advanced by the Japanese are generally more severe than those of other major donors. For a variety of reasons, therefore, a multilateral approach to aid and technical assistance in which the leading donor states of the Pacific basin cooperate has become imperative.

In summary, the economic component of U.S.-Japanese relations is at once vitally important and productive of complex problems. In many respects, our economic ties constitute the true foundation of our broader relations. They are particularly crucial to Japan, since her future prosperity depends heavily upon a continued healthy economic relation with the United States, and there are no real substitutes for this relation. But for the United States also such ties are very significant, affecting as they do outlets for our agricultural products, opportunities for our consumers to improve their standard of living, and the potential for an ever-widening program of technical and scientific interchange to the benefit of both societies.

Despite the importance of our bilateral relations in this sphere, such relations cannot be treated in isolation. To many issues and problems, multilateralism is the only feasible approach. Consequently, American-Japanese economic relations must be encased in a series of broader institutions and agreements. Some of these should pertain to the Pacific-Asian community, and go beyond mere trade and investment policies as these apply to advanced states. If we are to tackle the economic issues confronting the world as the twentieth century moves into its last quarter, no single level of approach alone will suffice. Unilateralism, bilateralism, and multilateralism must each play a part, together with a network of "North-South" agreements dedicated to reducing the gap between the haves and the have-nots.

We are now entering an age which requires new approaches to old problems. Nowhere will the results be more crucial than in the economic realm. The 1970s, therefore, should witness the development of new economic institutions as well as new policies, with the United States and Japan, as the foremost representatives of open economic systems, taking the lead.

THE POLITICAL DIMENSIONS OF U.S.-JAPANESE RELATIONS

If economic ties have constituted the foundations of the American-Japanese alliance, the political and military structure built upon that foundation is also of major importance, both to our two nations and to the rest of Asia. Let us now turn to the political dimensions of the American-Japanese relationship.

The Background of U.S.-Japanese Political Ties

As indicated earlier, Japan has repeatedly been confronted with the basic issues of continental involvement versus aloofness, alliance versus isolation. Historically, Japan abandoned isolation not out of desire but out of necessity. The West made its second entry into East Asia in the nineteenth century in insistent fashion, having acquired impressive power as a result of the industrial revolution. Once forced into contact, however, Japan quickly developed an interest in Western technology running alongside that historic xenophobia which continued to exist.

Then at the turn of the twentieth century, Japan found it in her interest to give up the policy of nonalignment and enter into a formal alliance with Great Britain, the most powerful state in the world at that time, so as to support Japanese policies in Asia. Armed with this alliance, Japan embarked upon a continental policy, with Korea the opening wedge. As we have noted, the Anglo-Japanese alliance lasted for two memorable decades, serving Japanese interests well until it was abandoned in favor of a weak multipolarism.

Once again, as World War II approached, Japan entered into an alliance — this time with Germany and Italy — another alliance outside of Asia to support policies in Asia. But on this occasion Japan's continental policies were to lead to overextension, confrontation with the United States, and total defeat. In 1945, Japan accepted American Occupation, having no other choice. Scarcely six years later, that same America proffered to Japan an alliance on exceedingly generous terms.

The reasons for this extraordinary turn of events are not difficult to discover. The premises underwriting the initial East Asian policies of the United States after 1945 all proved to be in error. Three themes had dominated American concepts of postwar Asia. First, a unified, democratic China under Nationalist rule and aided by the United States would provide the center around which the international relations of Asia would gravitate. Second, the United States and the Soviet Union, partners during World War II, could continue to reach satisfactory agreements and work together amicably. Third, the process of decolonization in South and Southeast Asia would be relatively quick and easy, with a number of independent states emerging, states dedicated to parliamentary, democratic political systems.

When each of these premises proved to be false, and the United States felt it necessary to use its own power in an effort to establish and maintain a political-military equilibrium in East Asia (as in Europe), it naturally looked for potential allies and supporters. The American-Japanese alliance was fashioned in the midst of the Korean War. From the beginning, it was an unequal alliance in the sense that the bulk of the power and of the commitments lay with the United States. Hence, it was a highly favorable alliance for Japan, given that nation's needs and capacities of the period. Having already underwritten Japan's economic rehabilitation, the United States now agreed to underwrite Japanese security, and in addition, to sponsor Japan as a member of the world community at a time when most World War II allies still favored harsh policies toward that nation.

What was the *quid pro quo*? Japan accepted American

bases, military installations that could be used in any conflict that might involve the United States in Asia. In a broader sense, moreover, Japan accepted membership in an American-oriented bloc. She became a part of a network of ties and alliances that included the Republic of Korea and the Republic of China on Taiwan in northeast Asia, and a number of other states in diverse parts of the world. On almost all political issues, Japan supported the United States both in the United Nations and in other settings.

From the beginning, internal opposition to this policy existed. The Japan Socialist Party fought bitterly against signing a separate peace treaty at San Francisco in 1951 without the approval of the Communist bloc, argued against the Mutual Security Treaty which was created at the same time, and urged a policy of neutralism for Japan, using Nehru's foreign policy as a model. The Socialists, however, remained a minority in the government, and judging from the public opinion polls of the early 1950s, a minority with respect to their basic foreign policy positions. The alliance with the United States had major advantages as long as America had both the power and will to maintain an international order largely through her own commitments. Japan was enabled to pursue a low risk foreign policy, with her resources devoted to economic growth.

Under the prevailing circumstances, Japan accepted a status vis-à-vis the United States not dissimilar from that pursued by Great Britain and West Germany, and for much the same reasons. None of these states in the aftermath of World War II could exercise political, economic, or military power independently. None of them wished to become a part of the Soviet bloc, and in each case, the political leadership regarded the risks and disadvantages of neutralism or nonalignment as decidedly greater than those of alliance with the United States.

Why, then, has a new debate opened in Japan concerning foreign policy, a debate within the Liberal Democratic Party as well as among other parties, and one speaking on occasion to basic issues? In our opening section, we have already suggested some of the broad factors motivating this debate. The central question is frequently posed as follows: in a period when the movement is from an American-centered toward a multipolar Asia, what is an appropriate foreign policy for Japan?

Attitudinal Changes in Japan and America

Before exploring the ramifications of this debate, let us look at certain subtle but vitally important changes that have taken place in what might be termed the psychological dimensions of the American-Japanese relationship. At the close of World War II, the United States was prepared psychologically, if not in many technical respects, to play a leadership role. Flushed with a massive military victory, confident of American institutions and the American way of life, and optimistic regarding the future, the occupational role came naturally — and as events would have it, proved to be highly successful. One reason for that success, moreover, related to the psychological mood of the Japanese in that era. Defeated, dispirited and disillusioned, the overwhelming majority of the Japanese people were prepared to accept a subordinate status. Tutelage at the hands of an external force proved not to be as wrenching an experience as might have been expected. Japanese xenophobia was suppressed by the urgent requirements of survival and the surprising generosity of the American occupiers.

From the outset of the postwar era, Americans and Japanese interacted remarkably well on a personal or group level, although true intimacy was rare indeed. The Americans were prepared to lead, the Japanese to follow. The quotients of openness and naiveté so manifest in the American character made an impact upon individuals accustomed to an intensely factionalized, rigidly hierarchical social system. In most respects, it was the attraction of opposites, the effective interaction of complementary cultures.

When the Japanese were polled on their attitudes toward Americans shortly after the occupation began, the response was strongly favorable. Among the "good points" of Americans cited, three predominated: generosity, openness or friendliness, and the capacity for hard work and efficiency. The weaknesses cited were also revealing: racial prejudice, boisterousness, and a disposition toward wastefulness. Americans were equally complimentary concerning Japanese, generally more favorably inclined to them than toward certain wartime allies. The Japanese traits particularly admired by Americans were their orderliness and discipline, cleanliness, work ethic, and high culture.

The psychological compatibility of our two peoples and cultures at that particular point in time should not be minimized as a factor making for a successful occupation, and beyond that, a successful alliance. Naturally, it was an alliance of unequals. But could Japan have accepted any other relationship? At home and abroad, the Japanese have conceived of relations in strongly hierarchical terms. Superior-inferior or inferior-superior relations have been vastly easier to establish and accept than those of equality.

Now, more than one-quarter of a century after World War II, psychological changes of far-reaching proportions appear to have occurred both among Americans and among Japanese. The American people seem weary, querulous, and uncertain of themselves. Gone, at least for the moment, are the qualities of buoyant optimism, self-assurance, and expansiveness that underwrote American leadership after

1945. Viewed in perspective, the new trends are completely understandable. Having borne heavy international burdens for three decades, often unilaterally, while at the same time consummating the greatest domestic revolution that the world has ever witnessed, a revolution affecting each citizen in his values, personal relations, mobility, and way of life, the American people have the same need for rest and recuperation as the soldier who has been fighting for weeks in the front lines.

Nevertheless, these changes in American psychology, implying as they do profound changes in American priorities, have evoked serious concern on the part of America's allies, including the Japanese. In the end, this concern frequently comes down to a single set of questions on the part of those basically committed to the American-Japanese alliance: Are American commitments credible? Do the American people have the stamina and the will at this point to play successfully a complex, sustained role in international politics when their interests or those of their allies are at stake?

In considerable part, of course, these are subjective questions, because "interests" are susceptible to varying definitions. As will shortly be discussed, various segments of the Japanese public and political elite do not regard their interests and perceived American interests as identical, or even compatible at this point. Beyond this, however, changes in the general psychological mood of the Japanese people add further complications. The achievements of Japan over recent decades, particularly in the economic field, have produced a heightened sense of self-confidence and independence. Fading is the old mood of despair and defeatism which helped to sustain a strong inferiority complex. The elements of paradox still abound in Japanese culture, as in most cultures,[12] but in the broadest sense, nationalism is returning to the Japanese scene, with its precise political manifestations yet unclear.

Thus, the psychological moods that tended to dominate our two peoples and elites at the beginning of the postwar era have undergone significant changes upon which moods feed. Admittedly, such generalizations are dangerous, the data to sustain them being difficult to obtain and easy to misinterpret. Let us look therefore at such data as exists in Japanese public opinion polls.

Recent Japanese Perceptions of Americans

What are the trends with respect to Japanese perceptions of conditions in the United States? During the decade of the 1960s, respect for the United States declined significantly if we may accept as accurate data derived from various polls.[13] In 1960, 62 percent of the Japanese public held a "good" or "very good" opinion of the United States. Only 35 percent held such opinions in 1969. Unfavorable impressions were especially pronounced on the following aspects of American life: American youth; the treatment of blacks; the extent of poverty in the United States; and the prevalence of crime and violence. This would indicate that the media, both Japanese and American, have had a major impact in shaping Japanese public attitudes toward "the facts" of American life, and in a generally adverse direction.

When somewhat broader aspects of American life were queried, the response was more positive. A strong majority (70 percent) looked favorably upon American cultural life and general living conditions. American education and the American economic system also received approval, albeit by reduced majorities (53 and 56 percent). But the American political system, together with American religion provoked a neutral response.

The stereotype of Americans among the Japanese as the decade of the 1960s came to a close was definitely a mixed one, considerably less favorable than in the immediate postwar period. A strong majority viewed Americans as "progressive," a trait considered good, and a fairly substantial minority saw them as "idealistic," but two other desirable traits — "hard working" and "sincere" — were now found lacking (12 and 8 percent respectively selected these as American traits). On the negative side, given Japanese cultural values, was materialism, although surprisingly perhaps, Americans were not seen as particularly warlike, lawless, or intolerant in the abstract — the answers here varying from the specific grievances noted above.

Troubled attitudes toward the United States are also reflected in another type of poll. For more than ten years, the Jiji Press has commissioned a nationwide monthly public opinion poll on the popularity of foreign nations. Until the mid-1960s, the United States held first place as the "most liked" country, with the percentage ranging from 44 to 49 percent. Beginning in 1965, American popularity slipped, and the United States fell into second place behind Switzerland, with percentages ranging from 41-32 between 1965 and 1970. Another major decline in American popularity took place in 1971, particularly in the last six months of that year, when the Jiji poll indicated that, as of November 1971, the United States was designated the "most liked" country by only 20 percent of the Japanese people, ranking fourth behind Switzerland (35 percent), the United Kingdom (26 percent), and France (26 percent).

The change in the percentage designating the United States as the "most disliked" nation has changed less, but here too, the trend is adverse. Prior to 1965, only 4-6 percent of Japanese put the United States in that category. Between 1965-1970, the average percentage so responding was about 8 percent. Between August and November 1971, roughly 11 percent so characterized the United States, with the high point in September (13 percent).

From the dates involved, we can construct the broad reasons for the shifts in Japanese public opinion. Clearly, the first decline, which began in 1965, is attributable to general adverse reactions to American policy in Vietnam. The even sharper decline taking place in 1971 can be attributed to a strongly negative attitude over the economic and political developments of the time, culminating in the "Nixon Shocks" of August 1971.

Thus, in the latter half of 1971, Japanese public opinion indicated a crisis of confidence in the American-Japanese alliance of major proportions. A poll taken by the semigovernmental Japan Broadcasting Corporation on September 26-27, 1971, indicated that predominant Japanese opinion foresaw the likelihood of some deterioration in U.S.-Japanese relations. Some 41 percent indicated that friendly relations would continue, but 48 percent predicted that friendly relations would weaken, including 20 percent who regarded confrontation as increasingly possible.[14]

When questioned as to why deterioration in U.S.-Japanese relations would take place, the principal reasons given related to economic friction, the American refusal to consult with Japan in the political field, and our military demands upon Japan, in order of significance.[15]

Most startling was a poll published by *Asahi* based upon December 1-2, 1971, interviews with 2,615 adults reportedly representative of the national electorate, and being the fourth poll (the first taken in September 1969) to ask the question, with which foreign country should Japan maintain the "closest friendly relations in the future?" The December 1971 poll indicated that while 28 percent of the respondents chose the United States, 33 percent chose the People's

Republic of China. This result was in striking contrast to the earlier polls, including that of May 1971, although a trend in the direction of China had commenced after the Cultural Revolution ended.[16]

Japanese Reactions to China and the Soviet Union

Before any conclusions are drawn from these polls, let us note attitudes toward China and the Soviet Union, as indicated by the Jiji poll cited earlier. While the Japanese public may desire closer relations with China, particularly in the immediate aftermath of the startling developments in Sino-American relations, a very small percentage regard China as their favorite nation. The Jiji poll of November 1971 indicated that only 5 percent listed China as the nation they liked most, exactly the same percentage as in 1961. Indeed, at no point throughout the 1961-1971 period did the percentage of China enthusiasts rise above 8 percent, and that figure was reached in a single month, that of September 1971, for reasons easy to discern. On the other hand, those considering China the "most disliked" nation, while still higher than those viewing the United States in that fashion, have declined significantly in the recent past. As of November 1971, 16 percent of the respondents were so recorded, compared to 26 percent during January-June 1971, 31 percent during 1970, a high point of 42 percent in 1967 (at the zenith point of the Cultural Revolution), and 32 percent in 1961. Compared to the past, therefore, China now occupies a less unfavorable position in Japanese public opinion, although it does not yet enjoy as favorable a positon as the United States, notwithstanding the successive drops in American popularity.

The Soviet Union clearly has more problems than any

other big power in establishing a positive image before the Japanese people. According to the Jiji poll, only 3 percent of the respondents in November 1971, claimed the Soviet Union as their "most liked" nation, and the high point for that view was 5 percent, achieved in 1961 and again in August and September 1971. In contrast, 28 percent of all respondents listed the Soviet Union as the "most disliked" nation in November 1971, making it the least popular of the major powers by a considerable margin. Indeed, the Soviet Union had been the most disliked power since the Jiji polls began in 1961, except for a brief time during the climax of the Cultural Revolution, when the Chinese People's Republic briefly took the booby prize. Dislike for Russia reached its high point in 1961-1962 when 44 and 46 percent of all respondents listed the U.S.S.R. as the "most disliked" nation. In the 1964-1969 period, the percentage so recording their views fluctuated between 39 and 37 percent, dropping to 33 percent in 1970.

Japanese Public Opinion and the Major Powers

There are good reasons to handle this poll data with caution. As has been noted, the questions are not always carefully balanced and put in neutral terms. Of equal importance, they are rarely related directly to specific events, or an appropriate context. Public opinion, finally, can be highly mercurial, especially when concentrated direction is given it. Nevertheless, the trends established by regular polls have significance. Perhaps the most important trends to be derived from the Jiji polls are these:

> 1. The United States is still the best liked among the major states of the Pacific-Asian region with whom Japan's fate is linked, but the

precipitous decline in its popularity in recent years can only be read as a serious warning sign for the American-Japanese alliance.

2. Opinions concerning China are highly volatile, suggesting a number of fierce, unresolved conflicts within the Japanese collective mind on this subject. Views can be dramatically swayed by specific incidents, but an ambivalence derived from the historical legacy, cultural proximity, and emotional involvement persists. Thus, with respect to public opinion, the China issue is likely to precipitate a lengthy struggle, with many turns in the road ahead.

3. The Soviet Union has none of the advantages of China when running in a popularity contest, a fact sharply underlined by the Jiji polls, and all other evidence. For the near future, at least, Soviet-Japanese rapprochement will have to rest upon other considerations.

4. It is to be noted that the nations "most liked" are all Western states. This signals the crucial fact that while the Japanese are an Asian people, they are also the people of an advanced, modern state, and many of their identifications are with similar peoples. More than ever, Japan draws her ideals if not her primary contacts from outside Asia.

At the same time, three of the four Western states most liked — and the first three — are European states with which Japan has quite minimal relations. In Switzerland, Great Britain, and France, Japanese see that combination of modernity, independence, and noninvolvement that strikes an appealing note. Their response

suggests the desire for a minimal foreign policy —
and hence for countries making minimal demands
upon Japan.

In contrast, the nations disliked most are
without exception Asian states close at hand
(including the Soviet Union). Two of them are the
Communist giants whose territories extend near to
Japanese shores. But one, the Republic of Korea
(always prominent on the negative side of the
roster), indicates that ideological or policy considerations are not the only factors that can
influence Japanese public opinion adversely.
Toward both the Koreans and the Russians, racial
feelings inject themselves into the picture, although
it might be equally appropriate to call these
feelings "cultural antipathies."

5. In recent years, a steadily increasing number
of Japanese have been unwilling to indicate any
nation as "most liked" or "most disliked,"
signaling a rise in "Japan-first" sentiments, stronger commitments to autonomy and aloofness,
attitudes betokening an increase in Japanese
nationalism.

Foreign Policy and the Japanese Parties

Although its importance has grown in recent years, public
opinion in Japan can scarcely be considered a controlling
element in the making of Japanese foreign policy, particularly since elections have been determined by issues of
domestic policy in Japan as elsewhere. Let us examine elitist
positions, therefore, briefly turning to the political parties as
the first sample. Here, we can use official policy statements
and public utterances of party spokesmen as a reasonably

accurate gauge of the views of the majority of the party leadership.

The Japan Socialist Party can claim to be the leading opposition party, with the support of about one-quarter of the Japanese people.[17] Throughout the last decade, the Socialists have been dominated by their left wing. On issues of foreign policy, while they remain officially committed to a policy of neutrality, pacifism, and "friendly relations with all nations," in fact, their views and positions on specific issues are governed by a strident anti-Americanism and a growing commitment to united front politics in conjunction with the Asian Communists and their allies.

Currently, the China issue and the questions of U.S.-Japan security arrangements preoccupy Socialist leaders. On China, they call for the abrogation of the Japan-Republic of China treaty, and the conclusion of a treaty with the People's Republic of China based upon Peking's three political principles and the five principles of peaceful coexistence. At an appropriate time, moreover, they envisage the signing of a Sino-Japanese Treaty of Mutual Friendship and Non-aggression as a partial substitute for the current Mutual Security Treaty with the United States. This would be preceded by "a movement" dedicated to Japanese-Chinese friendship as part of "the struggle against militarist revival in Japan" and "American imperialism."[18]

The party strongly opposes any military defenses or political arrangements involving Japan, South Korea, and Taiwan. It insists that the Japan-Republic of Korea treaty be abolished, that diplomatic relations be established with the Democratic People's Republic of Korea (North Korea), and that support be given the Communist proposals for a unified Korea. It accepts Peking's position on the Taiwan issue completely, and urges that all political relations with Taiwan be severed. It supports the Democratic Republic of Vietnam

(North Vietnam) position with respect to Vietnam and Indochina. The agreement concerning Okinawan reversion is opposed, because through it, Okinawa is incorporated into the Japan-U.S. security system, and, argues the JSP, can be used as a base for all weapons, including nuclear ones despite assurances to the contrary, since a thorough inspection of American military facilities will not be allowed. These stands on specific issues do not preclude the party from insisting that its ultimate goal is pacifism *and* neutrality.[19]

On the Soviet issue, considerable caution is exercised by the Socialists, indicative of the strong pull of Peking upon the party mainstream. Several high-level official trips to Moscow have been undertaken by party officials, however, with some degree of accord announced. Party spokesmen favor normalization of relations with the Soviet Union, but have not made this one of their highest priority issues.

To capture the flavor of Socialist public rhetoric, one can turn to the remarks of Kawasaki Kanji, director of the party's International Bureau, at the time of his visit with Sihanouk in Peking, January 5, 1972.[20] Kawasaki asserted that the Socialist Party "is determined to drive American imperialism out of Japan, and through the struggle, to aim at Japan's true independence and autonomy, peace, neutrality and prosperity; to advance solidarity with the struggles to oppose the United States and save their countries being carried out by the Cambodian people and the peoples of the three Indochina states."

Concerning the Nixon trip to Peking, Kawasaki asserted, "The Nixon trip to Peking has been described (by the North Koreans) as Nixon raising the white flag. We also think that this is a correct appraisal."[21]

As will be noted, current Socialist foreign policy positions are diametrically opposed to the major policies being pursued by the Japanese government, and it is difficult to distinguish

JSP pronouncements from those of Peking, P'yŏngyang or Hanoi on a wide range of issues. The Socialists adhere to "neutrality" as an abstraction, but on most concrete policy issues they stand with, or close to the position of the Asian Communists, defending that stance generally on nationalist grounds.

Curiously, the Japan Communist Party is bitterly anti-Maoist at present, and as a result, it has recently moved closer to Moscow. This has not always been true. In the Comintern-Cominform era, of course, the JCP was a loyal supporter of the Soviet line. By the early 1960s, however, the party stood with Peking in oppositon to Khrushchev's policies. But events in 1966 involving Mao's refusal to support a joint Communist campaign of assistance in North Vietnam soured the JCP leadership on Mao, and the Cultural Revolution did nothing to improve matters. The JCP then entered a period of strongly asserting its independence, adopting a "plague on both your houses" approach to Peking and Moscow. More recently, however, the Russians have made gains in their efforts to improve relations with their Japanese comrades.

Current JCP foreign policy pronouncements reflect these facts. The attack on the Chinese People's Republic is blunt and direct. JCP leaders accuse "the Mao Tse-tung faction" of having tried to interfere in the internal affairs of the JCP for five years in an effort to destroy its leadership.[22] China is accused of pursuing policies of "socialist colonialism" under the guise of cooperation with other parties and nationalist groupings.[23] The Nixon trip, moreover, was handled in a very different manner by the Communists than by the Socialists. "The Chinese side did not treat Nixon as the prime mover of aggression, but accepted him as the Chief of State of America, and extended a friendly welcome to him. Nixon visited China flying the Stars and Stripes and the Nixon Doctrine, and not a white flag at all."[24]

Despite its antagonism to the present Chinese regime, however, the JCP takes a position of "non-intervention" with respect to the Sino-Soviet dispute, using this stand to advance the case for noninterference in its own affairs. Nevertheless, it is now strongly championing the cause of improved relations between Japan and the Soviet Union. The issue of the northern territories, the JCP insists, can be solved, particularly if Japan will abandon her security ties with the United States, substituting for them a policy of neutrality.

There are no surprises in the Communist attitude toward the American-Japanese alliance. The choice for Japan in the 1970s, proclaims the party, is between a revival of Japanese militarism subordinated to the United States and the creation of a "united front of peace, neutrality and democracy."[25] The Security Treaty must be dissolved, together with all other special ties connecting the United States and Japan. Changes in foreign policy can only be effected through a rolling revolution in Japan itself. The first stage will be the creation of a "democratic coalition government" which will not itself be a revolutionary regime, but will function until such a regime can emerge, with its mission to abrogate the U.S.-Japan Security Treaty and move Japan toward an "anti-imperialist united front."

The divisions within the Japanese "Left" over foreign policy at present pertain mainly to the radically different views held by Socialists and Communists over China, and more specifically, the Maoist regime. A portion of the more moderate elements within the JSP, moreover, has qualms about united front operations, given ultimate Communist goals. Nevertheless, on a wide range of specific policies, cooperation has been effected and united front politics strongly appeals to the Socialist Left.

The Komeito, (Clean Government Party), a party based upon a Buddhist religious sect, Soka Gakkai, aspires to the original Socialist position of strict neutrality. Its chairman, Takeiri Yoshikatsu, recently proclaimed its basic policy as one of "complete neutrality" and "an equal distance" between it and each of the major states – the United States, China, and Russia. He asserted that only the Komeito leaders could visit each of these nations and be received cordially and with respect.[26] From its position on specific issues, however, the Komeito acquires a certain Asia-centrism, foreseeing a special economic, cultural, and political role for Japan as an *Asian* nation. It supports an early dissolution of the Mutual Security Treaty and the complete evacuation of U.S. bases from Okinawa. It would substitute a multilateral guarantee of Japan's security by the major powers, with defense expenditures being kept to minimal levels and "friendly relations with all states," but with an emphasis upon Japanese-Chinese ties.

The Komeito insists that the China issue is the most important one confronting Japan, and advocates normalization of relations with the CPR at the earliest possible time, based on an acceptance of Peking's position that Taiwan is a province of the People's Republic, and entirely an internal matter; thus, the Japan-Republic of China Treaty is illegal and must be voided.

Komeito leaders have sharply criticized the Sato government for failing to perceive "the disintegration of the bipolar system" at an earlier point, and clinging to dependence upon the United States when the goal should have been "autonomous diplomacy."[27]

The Democratic Socialist Party comes closest among opposition parties to supporting the foreign policies of the government as these have evolved in recent years. Its objections are to specific elements within those policies more than to the broad policies themselves, and also to the timing of changes in light of the altered international scene. Thus, it proclaims itself "not opposed to the United States," and hence able to speak frankly on such problems as Okinawan reversion, normalization of relations with China, and the future security structure. On Okinawa, its position has been that nonnuclear principles should be applied, as to Japan proper, and that a schedule should be publicly established for the reduction of bases.

Until late 1971, the DSP position on the China-Taiwan issue was that the Peking government represented China, and Taiwan was an internal problem of China, but that any solution "ought to respect the will of the Taiwanese."[28] By early 1972, however, the DSP had abandoned the desire to protect the rights of the Taiwanese, and had indicated its willingness to cut ties with Taiwan. The DSP position on the U.S.-Japan Security Treaty is that it should gradually be revised, with American forces withdrawing from Asia, but only as tension is decreased in the area, and with Japanese security ultimately being guaranteed via an autonomous defense program based upon a carefully restricted Japanese Defense Force together with such international agreements as can be obtained.

Within the Liberal Democratic Party itself, however, may lie the trends of greatest importance, because this party still commands more support than any of the opposition elements, and it is destined to govern Japan for the near future at least. Increasingly, in recent years, significant differences over foreign policy issues have emerged within the LDP. In some cases, these differences have been generated by rival factions in the party to garner the support of the public or particular special interests. One cannot assume that the leader of a victorious faction or coalition of factions would act in office as he speaks prior to office. Nevertheless, several basic issues have figured prominently in intraparty debates, suggesting the new tides affecting Japanese conservatives.[29]

China has been a prime issue for a number of years. The official position of the government has been that Japan is not in a position to speak of Taiwan, since it waived all rights and powers over that island under the San Francisco Peace Treaty. However, the Japanese government "can fully understand Peking's claim that Taiwan is a part of the Chinese People's Republic." This later statement is close to the one successfully employed by several other governments in establishing relations with the C.P.R. Thus far, however, Peking has adamantly rejected this position, demanding an unequivocal acceptance of the C.P.R.'s stand prior to formal negotiations. The question of a peace treaty with China, and specifically, the provisions it might contain, constitute another subject of debate.

Meanwhile, some party leaders have established independent channels of communication with Peking and, in a number of cases, they have signalled a willingness to accept the Peking position on the Taiwan issue as the price for normalized relations. Despite the sizeable contingent within the LDP that remains strongly opposed to any "capitulation" on the Taiwan issue, no question has divided party ranks so deeply as this one, especially since the new turns in American-Chinese relations have come to be known.[30]

Issues pertaining to Japan's territorial claims have also been the subject of periodic debate within the party, notably the position to be taken on Okinawa and the northern territories. The differences have related to the degree of toughness and determination desirable to secure Japanese interests. Attitudes toward the allocation of responsibilities between Japan and the United States on defense matters, possible revison of the Mutual Security Treaty, defense expenditures versus social welfare outlays, and relations with the divided states of Korea and Vietnam have all evoked a range of opinions, reflecting uncertainties about the broader course to be pursued.

As can readily be seen, even when the Liberal Democratic Party acts as a unified entity, Japanese foreign policy must operate under the handicap of an absence of consensus, both on specific issues and on the most basic principles. The differences between the Liberal Democrats and the Socialists, for example, could scarcely be more profound. In the past, this has not been a major problem only because the Liberal Democratic Party has held power uninterruptedly since Japan secured its independence in 1951, and on basic policy issues it has remained united. Few nations in the world have enjoyed the degree of political stability present in Japan, and unquestionably, this has been one factor abetting the phenomenal economic growth of the society.

Political Trends and Their Impact on Japanese Foreign Policy

Will such stability continue in the decade ahead? This is by no means certain. One of the seeming paradoxes of recent years is that in the midst of a burgeoning prosperity, signs of political instability have gradually accumulated in Japan. Rapid economic growth and increasing affluence, far from being conducive to a strengthening of the moderate-conservatives, have generated those issues and attitudes that provide a threat to their unity and power.

The problems of urbanism reach their most acute forms in Japan, partly as a result of the extraordinarily rapid growth of the last decade and the limited space available for expansion. Thus, as we have seen, the issue of governmental priorities has been raised directly, especially as it pertains to the domestic scene. This, in turn, has acted as a further deterrent to any foreign policy that would enlarge costs and risks, hence aggravating the divisions within LDP ranks in the aftermath of an uncertain American posture and image in Asia.

Recent elections have reflected these factors. Despite the major LDP victory in the House of Representatives' elections of December, 1969, in terms of number of seats gained, the LDP percentage of the popular vote dropped and this has been a more or less continuous trend. The party has exhibited particular weakness in metropolitan areas, reflective of the growing frustrations of the big city dweller. As is indicated in the December 1971 *Asahi* poll quoted above, the LDP appears to be at the lowest point (42 percent) in the years during which this particular poll has been taken.
been taken.

The situation is made more uncertain because of the growing fissures among the LDP factions, hence the possibility of a major split and subsequent realignment of political forces. In addition to divisions over issues, generational differences are becoming increasingly apparent within the party. The evidence suggests that a potentially significant shift is at hand from the type of conservative leadership epitomized by Yoshida Shigeru, Kishi Nobuske, and his brother, Sato Eisaku, to a new, "postwar" generation. The former men were typical of those whose initial training and experience came from the prewar era, men of the bureaucracy, and of a time when Japan found it in her interests to concentrate heavily upon economic growth. Now, postwar men stand in the wings, waiting impatiently to assume power, and it is by no means clear as to how they will think and act, but some changes of style and direction are likely. The by-word is "more dynamism." A changing of the guard is at hand within the Liberal Democratic Party — if not now, certainly within this decade.[31]

Political instability would be a virtual certainty for Japan at this point were the opposition parties stronger or more united, yet none of these parties have gained noticeably in public esteem despite LDP slippage. And the difficulties in forming a reliable coalition based upon the opposition parties remain formidable, notwithstanding successful joint efforts on a few issues.

Coalition government in Japan at some point during the 1970s, however, cannot be ruled out. Such a coalition would not necessarily be based solely upon the opposition parties. Indeed, a more likely possibility would appear to be a coalition involving one or more factions of the Liberal Democratic Party, groups breaking away from the main stream and seeking to establish themselves as the governing body with opposition cooperation. That effort might already have been attempted had not the Japanese electoral procedures discouraged it. It may be tried, however, despite the risks involved for the breakaway group.

It is also possible that, in the future as in the past, the Liberal Democratic Party will successfully adjust to the pressures and demands emanating from Japanese society, and contain political change within its own ranks via a series of alterations in leadership, organization, and policies. Even if this proves to be true, however, an increased element of uncertainty is inevitable, given the times and the issues. In sum, the signs point to a greater degree of political instability in Japan in the years ahead, and that could have a major impact upon foreign policy, probably one on balance disadvantageous to Japan. In any case, the premium will continue to be upon a foreign policy that runs limited risks and evokes limited protest, with an increased attention to the domestic problems that have resulted from dramatically successful economic growth.

The Impact of the Japanese Media

One additional factor likely to abet political instability warrants notice, namely, the mass media. In general, the Japanese media, and particularly the press, have betrayed a strong antigovernment bias. This is notably true of Japan's largest and most influential newspaper, *Asahi,* which tends to an anti-American, leftist position reflective of a majority of its writers, and is normally highly critical of governmental policies, both foreign and domestic.

The influence of the press on Japanese public opinion and also on political circles is substantial, as the polling data indicates, especially in the arena of foreign policy. It has just come to light, incidentally, that a portion of the press, including *Asahi*, have since 1964 been committed to an acceptance of Peking's "three political principles" as a condition of being allowed to station newsmen in Peking, suggesting the type of problems that currently exist in the Japanese press.[32]

Concerns and Responses Between Japanese and Americans

Against this background, let us turn to the central political alternatives with which Japan is faced in the international realm. Before suggesting these, however, it is essential to signal the major concerns currently being voiced in Japanese political and intellectual circles. Through them, we can better discern the mood of a nation increasingly troubled by a sense of uncertainty, even confusion, in the face of the dramatic political changes of recent years in the Pacific-Asian region.

Will Japan be isolated by a new tripolar politics in Asia,

with the United States, the Soviet Union, and China, being given the principal roles? No single political issue has evoked greater concern. The new politics, it is argued, is based essentially upon a pragmatic, hard-headed, nonideological balance of power through which each large state expects to realize its national interests. Everywhere, it is asserted, nationalism is triumphing in international relations, with the premium upon self-interest and the skillful interweaving of power in all of its forms to serve national goals. Is not the United States in the process of abandoning its special relation to Japan, its words of assurance notwithstanding, and, indeed, giving up all of those alliances based upon an earlier, less refined balance of power concept in the bipolar era?

Under the circumstances now prevailing, how can Japan insure her own interests? Without significant military power and lacking political stature, Japan is likely to find most coalitions excluding her or operating against her. Does her economic power alone constitute sufficient leverage, or will other weapons be necessary? Has the position of the United States been distorted by unfriendly sources in the aftermath of "the Nixon shocks," and does the alliance still retain its significance?

Both the geography and the political culture of Japan make the Japanese highly susceptible to recurrent fears of (and desires for) isolation. An island community, Japan possesses a remarkably homogeneous culture, and one that has retained a surprising portion of its integrity despite the inroads of modernity. Moreover, the Japanese are a people introverted and private, in whom the sense of not belonging to the wider world wells up repeatedly, and for whom emotional questions of trust or betrayal, obligation or abandonment remain important.

Hence, some very personal considerations also constitute matters of concern to the Japanese elite at present. Is there an anti-Japanese prejudice in the topmost echelons of the American government today? Are certain stereotypes about Japan and Japanese political behavior implanted in the mind of Dr. Henry Kissinger and possibly, the President himself? Privately, this issue has been discussed in high Japanese circles for nearly three years, long before the crises of 1971. It remains a troublesome, unresolved doubt. Meanwhile, the problem of treating others as equals, the trauma involved in breaking away from inferior-superior or superior-inferior relationships remains acute.

Japanese commentators, it should be quickly stated, are not loathe to criticize their own society in terms far harsher than those used publicly or privately by any American. For example, one analysis frequently advanced is that current American-Japanese difficulties stem in considerable measure from the rise of a narrow nationalism in Japan which sustains a concept of independent, self-centered action in the international arena without principle, and based solely upon materialist considerations. Japan has behaved like an economic animal, forsaking mutuality and placing a narrow concept of immediate gain before all else, it is asserted. Hence, a growing distrust of Japan on the part of the United States developed naturally, spurred on by the increasingly aloof character of the Ikeda and Sato governments. Support to the United States on issues of critical importance was given begrudgingly or not at all, at least until it was forced by dramatic moves like those of August 15, 1971.

Criticisms from within Japan of this nature, let it be reiterated, are not rare, and they are consistent with complaints frequently voiced in the United States. Trenchant criticisms of American policy have also increased in Japan, however, publicly and privately. It is often alleged that a cold Machiavellian quality now dominates U.S. foreign policy, drawn consciously or unconsciously from a nineteenth century European model. Thus, a willingness is exhibited to set aside special ties like those with Japan for a perception of American national interests as being best served when an equal distance is maintained from all other states, irrespective of historical, economic or institutional-ideological factors. Hence, the concept of equidistant multipolarism supported by elements like the Komeito, obtains additional support from Japanese perceptions of current American thought and policy. It is further asserted that American policy shifts, geared primarily to domestic considerations, have been so abrupt and conducted in such a style as to render satisfactory adjustment by allies like Japan virtually impossible. Those who earlier supported the United States are thus placed on the defensive, their political positions severely weakened.

To these separate allegations, responses have been forthcoming. Those defending Japanese policies, as noted earlier, often admit that appropriate adjustment to Japan's newly developed economic power was belated, but in most respects, protectionism was no more extensive than in West Europe. After 1968, moreover, the shift toward free trade has been as rapid as in any nation of the advanced world, with the more thorny problems of capital liberalization and monetary policies also receiving attention despite domestic opposition of an intense nature. On the political front, it is submitted, Japan at considerable cost has in the past supported the United States on such issues as Vietnam, China-Taiwan, and a host of other difficult problems. To pursue an independent course at this point on some issues, however, is essential both from the standpoint of the domestic political scene and from the standpoint of the continued health of Japan-U.S. relations.

From the American side comes an equally strong rejoinder to the criticisms set forth above. President Nixon and all other officials, it is asserted, have repeatedly made it clear that United States-Japan ties continue to be regarded by the American government as of critical importance, more vital than those with any other nation in the Pacific-Asian area. American public opinion, moreover, contrary to recent trends within the Japanese public, supports this view. Allegations concerning the abruptness of American policy changes are refuted with respect to economic matters, acknowledged but partially defended with regard to political (China) developments. For some years, it is pointed out, the United States implored Japan to take seriously the inequities in our economic relations, but to little or no avail. Measures short of dramatic ones appeared likely to fail, and the American domestic scene required urgent, forceful action.

On the political front, it is argued, rapid changes were also mandatory if the isolationist tide were to be stemmed, and if new avenues toward peaceful coexistence were to be opened. Complete secrecy regarding the initial moves toward the People's Republic of China, moreover, was essential since their success was by no means assured, and a publicized failure would have been far worse than having made no attempt at all. In no case, it is added, were Japanese interests bartered away in the negotiations with Chinese leaders, nor were any agreements injurious to Japan reached. On the contrary, our special ties to Japan were restated and defended in the course of the China talks. Nevertheless, apologies have recently been tendered for American unilateralism, with pledges that it will not recur.

The United States, it is contended, does not object to a more autonomous diplomacy by Japan, regarding this as a natural step in the evolution of both Japan and Asia at this point. Indeed, in certain respects, the United States has consciously abetted Japanese movement in that direction. America is no longer prepared to assume the preponderate burdens and responsibilities in our mutual relations. It not only accepts but insists upon a greater equity in these relations, realizing that this will involve continuous discussions and compromises over our respective interests.

Indeed, some quarters feel that in effect, the United States is abetting significant Japanese rearmament by encouraging a more independent Japanese foreign policy. To support rearmament directly, according to this view, would be counterproductive for America. However, the logic of the Nixon Doctrine is that Japanese power must be brought into play in Asia if a meaningful balance of power is to be attained, and the burdens of the United States reduced.

The concerns and responses set forth here constitute a part of the ongoing dialogue between the United States and Japan. More accurately, perhaps, they underlie that dialogue and represent an element in the stream of consciousness of both parties. Out of this atmosphere, three broad political positions have emerged in Japan, or are in the course of being formulated. To these, let us now turn.

Basic Political Alternatives for Japan

The first position we may define as the neutralist position, an old stand now acquiring new support. The neutralists posit as desirable the movement of Japan from alliance to nonalignment. Using the theme of "friendly relations with all nations," Japan would create a foreign policy based upon an equal distance from each major power. The foundations of such a policy would rest upon the substitution of a multipower guarantee of Japanese security for the Mutual Security Treaty; the acceptance of the lowest level of Japanese military power consistent with "self-defense" defined in the most minimal terms; the rapid normalization of relations with both the Chinese People's Republic and the Soviet Union, and with other states now excluded from

Japan's diplomatic lists for political reasons; and the projection of a Japanese international role based upon economic power, with such cultural and political inputs into the international scene as flow naturally from that power.

The arguments advanced on behalf of this policy can be anticipated. With the decline of bipolarism, and more particularly, with the reduction of the American commitment and capacity in Asia, it is asserted, a Japan-United States alliance no longer serves Japanese interests. It becomes both antiquated and dangerous, tieing Japan to a past era. The United States cannot be depended upon to defend Japanese interests, should they be threatened, either in military or in economic-political terms. On the contrary, the element of competition, even antagonism, will inevitably grow between these two nations. Meanwhile, special ties with America will make Japan an extended target, bringing down upon her periodic attacks from other major states in the area, raising the risks of her involvement in conflict and making any normalization of relations with the Communist states infinitely more difficult.

Neither China nor Russia pose a real threat to Japan, it is argued, nor are their basic policies necessarily a challenge to Japanese interests. Hence, if Japan can withdraw from the "Cold War" alliance system centering upon the United States and its small allies and establish a relation of complete equity with all states irrespective of their economic-political systems, it will have achieved a foreign policy carrying even more minimal risks than in the past, and promising still greater gains.

Any dependence upon military power, it is asserted, not only jeopardizes Japan's relations with the Communist states in her near vicinity, but also raises problems with the states of Southeast Asia with whom she hopes to carry out extensive economic relations. Military power, including nuclear weapons, has not given Great Britain or France a major voice in international politics, nor does such power suffice to protect overseas markets. Given the nature of military technology in the late twentieth century, moreover, only continental-mass societies can achieve real military credibility in the big power league. Japan must depend upon its economic capacities, and upon the emergence of a complex multipolar equilibrium in which each of the major powers will have a stake.

As indicated earlier, neutralism or nonalignment serves on occasion as a camouflage for elements of the Left who in fact have deep ideological and political commitments to one side of the political spectrum and in some cases at least, regard neutralism merely as a tactic, preparatory to a new alignment. True neutrality as an attitude is exceedingly difficult to achieve and maintain, even in an age widely proclaimed as nonideological, pragmatic, and oriented around the achievement of "national interest" objectives. When attitudes are too "unneutral," moveover, as in the case of the Japanese Left Socialists and Communists, they affect the credibility of a policy formally designated as "nonaligned." Nevertheless, neutralism as a basic position now appeals to a sizeable number of Japanese not affiliated with the Left, some of the arguments presented above having a strong impact.

The arguments against neutralism continue to be advanced vigorously. With Japan's economic and political ties destined to be primarily with the advanced, democratic states in the future, as in the past, how can an effort to have "equidistant" relations with such states as the People's Republic of China and the Soviet Union serve Japanese interests? Such a policy, it is asserted, is not only unrealistic, but so indicative of opportunism that it will create ineradicable suspicion and hostility from the United States and other states with which Japan currently has special relations, thereby producing great damage to Japan's true interests. Nor is there any evidence at present, it is charged, that China and Russia are prepared to accept a relationship of equals, and operate on matters economic, political and military, in a reciprocal fashion. Even if attempted, "neutralism" would be a one-way street.

A second position recently showing signs of increasing vitality can be labelled the pan-Asian position. Once again, its major themes are scarcely new, having roots that go deeply into the Japanese past, including the more recent past – the decade of the 1930s. The pan-Asian view in its purest form is that Japan should center its primary commitments and most intimate relations upon East Asia, acknowledging that by tradition, culture and desire, it is an *Asian* nation, and that only with other Asians, can it find its true identity and long-range role.

The pan-Asian argument is that the Western-oriented international position into which Japan gravitated after World War II is an unnatural one brought about as a result of military defeat and the advent of an American era in the Pacific-Asian region. Necessarily, it produced a subordination of Japan to Western values and standards as well as to Western power. At root, however, the affinities of the Japanese people are still with the Asian people, and particularly with people like the Chinese who come from a common cultural heritage. The mistakes made by Japan when she pursued pan-Asianism in the 1930s should not preclude a return to policies sanctioned by the natural bonds among peoples linked intimately together through racial, cultural and historic ties. Irrespective of current ideological differences, peoples like the Japanese and the Chinese understand each other far more profoundly than can ever be the case in Japanese-American relations.

Once again, pan-Asianism finds support from a diversity of sources. Avant-garde radicals join with traditionalists in paying homage to it, with both the motives and the degree of support varying. The opposition to pan-Asianism is also formidable. Japan, it is asserted, is as much a Western as an Asian state − possibly more so. Its economic development, its political institutions, its modern culture all give to the contemporary Japanese citizen more basic links to societies in roughly comparable stages of development than to those nations with which it shares merely historic ties and geographic propinquity. This is likely to be even more true of the future, since Japan's fate is increasingly tied with that of the advanced world. Even the critical issues of war or peace, prosperity or depression in Asia relate centrally to relations among the major states, Asian *and* Western. Thus, it is hopelessly romantic to attempt a reconstruction of policies based upon old myths, long since antedated. It is also a not-so-subtle form of racism.

Despite these arguments, the pan-Asian position plays a role in shaping attitudes and policy proposals, especially toward China. The importance of racial feelings in Japan, and their influence upon political attitudes, should not be lightly dismissed, moreover, either at grassroots or elitist levels.

A third position can be defined as that of modified alliance. This position accepts the need for a more independent diplomacy, and an adjustment to the advent of a multipolar Asia. However, its adherents regard the retention of close ties, both economic and political-security, with the United States as best suited to Japanese interests in the years immediately ahead. According to proponents of a continued Japan-U.S. alliance, such a policy need not preclude separate policies on certain issues, nor the normalization of relations with either China or the U.S.S.R.

The arguments on behalf of modified alliance commence

with the thesis that close relations between Japan and the United States flow naturally from the vital nature of their economic ties, the sharing of common political institutions and values, and in a broader sense, the capacity to interact meaningfully on a wide range of problems connected with rapid modernization. Sentiment, they insist, cannot be substituted for an appreciation of the realities of the current world, and those realities dictate much closer relations between Japan and the United States than with a still backward, ideologically rigid, largely closed China or with a powerful, highly nationalistic, antiliberal Russia. The presence of problems between allies is natural, say the supporters of modified alliance, but the solutions lie in tackling the specific issues at stake and working toward more successful institutions of consultation and interaction, not in drifting into an isolationist position, or attempting to apply the unrealistic notion of an equidistant stance before all nations.

It is further argued that as long as Japan proposes to make its basic international commitment in the economic field and eschew major military power, an alliance with the United States remains highly desirable. Only with such ties can Japan avoid total dependence upon the good will of the Communist nuclear powers. The U.S.-Japan alliance helps to prevent a greater resort to blackmail, and even provides Japan with some additional leverage in her dealings with Peking and Moscow. Moreover, the terms of the alliance, generous in the past, need not be onerous in the future.

The arguments against a modified alliance with the United States have already been presented, in the main, in connection with a discussion of the other two major positions. In summary, it is charged that any type of alliance with the United States reduces Japan's independence, drives her into commitments inconsistent with her own interests, increases the risks of involvement in regional or international conflict, and rests upon the dubious assumption that American pledges are credible.

We have outlined these three positions as pure types, whereas in reality, they rarely present themselves in that form, existing rather as moods, views and partial positions, with a goodly element of mixture and inconsistency on the scene. We should delineate two additional positions, moreover, less prevalent but existent in the total spectrum of views currently held among Japanese.

A fourth position can be called the Gaullist position, a commitment to an independent position based upon military as well as economic power, and aiming at protection of Japanese interests by securing admission into the nuclear club. Those holding this position would take the risks of major power status in order to secure what they believe to be its benefits in an age still dominated by factors of power and status.

The Gaullist advocates insist that as long as Japan lacks an independent military capacity, including the possession of nuclear weapons, she will be dependent upon foreign states, and that in the coming decade such dependence will result in Japanese interests being disregarded, policies crucial to Japan being abruptly changed without adequate consultation, Japanese complaints going unheeded, and the advent of recurrent crises, some of them the products of successfully applied blackmail to Japan, in which Japan will invariably lose.

Gaullist arguments include these theses: that American guarantees are no longer credible, and in any case, American and Japanese interests are marked by a growing divergence; that Chinese objectives are to contain Japan, keeping it militarily impotent, politically insignificant, and − ultimately − economically disadvantaged, goals not to be countered by bargaining from weakness; and that the Soviet Union has always pursued a policy of making minimal concessions to its opponents, especially Japan, with its bargaining hinged only to strength.

The arguments against the Gaullist position will be examined more closely at a later point. Suffice it to note here that they range from the assertion that Gaullism has failed in all of its major objectives in France, the nation of its birth, to the thesis that there are more types of power than military power, and a militarily strong Japan would forfeit significant economic and political advantages without acquiring a credible deterrent capacity in the military field.

To institute a Gaullist policy would require a considerable political shift, both of leadership and of public sentiment. As we shall indicate later, as long as the perception of external threat to Japan remains low and American security pledges retain some of their validity in Japanese eyes, support for the Gaullist position will remain low. In looser, vaguer terms, however, Gaullism has an undeniable appeal and, indeed, it is found in each of the major positions outlined above, since it represents one form of a nationalism long submerged.

A final position is that of the united front, a commitment to a union of "Left" forces dedicated to the liberation movement and to a Socialist future for Asia. The advocates of this position argue that Japan must become a part of the "newly emerging forces," to borrow an old Sukarno phrase. They seek to commit the nation in its foreign as in its domestic policies to an "anti-capitalist," "anti-imperialist" stance in company with other "progressive" forces, especially in Asia.

As we have seen, this position is espoused (albeit, with critical differences as to allies and enemies) not merely by the Japanese Communists, but also by a significant portion of the Socialists. Under present circumstances, however, it has a very limited following as a "pure" position, and is primarily important as it infiltrates the neutralist and pan-Asian positions earlier set forth.

Japan's China Dilemma

How do these basic positions, reflecting as they do radically different philosophic judgments as well as sharply variant assessments of the state of the current world and the nature of Japan's own interests, influence the concrete policies that Japan pursues or contemplates toward the major powers? Let us look first at the troublesome China issue.

Unquestionably, China currently represents the most frustrating problem within the entire foreign policy spectrum for the Sato government. Ideally, that government would like to shift its diplomatic relations from Taipei to Peking while retaining economic ties with Taiwan. It would also like to see the continuance of an independent Taiwan, separate from the control of the People's Republic of China. C.P.R. control over Taiwan would not only be likely to have adverse economic repercussions for Japan, but more importantly, it would signal the advent of the Chinese People's Republic as a Pacific power, with the need for naval and aerial strength to patrol the China sea and beyond. Thus, Japan would ultimately find China standing astride its main routes by sea and air to the south; the vital arteries of trade upon which its life depends.

Peking's leaders are fully aware of the Japanese government's private views and concerns. They are equally determined to prevent policies akin to those just sketched from coming to pass. One of the central objectives of Chinese policy at present is to contain Japan both politically and militarily. The threat of "Japanese militarism" ranks scarcely behind that of "Soviet revisionism" and "American imperialism," and as Chou En-lai has made clear in numerous interviews, the time to prevent Japan from being a major political or military force in the Pacific is now.

Several years ago, Peking discerned what it conceived to be the official American-Japanese scenario for Northeast Asia: the United States would gradually withdraw from the forward positions which it occupied in Northeast Asia, but it would hand to Japan the task of providing the bulk of the economic, political and military support necessary for the survival of an independent South Korea and Taiwan. In effect, a NEATO (Northeast Asia Treaty Organization) would thus be created, and the prospects of a unified Korea under Communist control, or the incorporation of Taiwan into China would be greatly diminished. On the other hand, if Japan could be precluded from playing this role, an ultimate Chinese supremacy in the region would be probable, with Japan confined to her four main islands, and dependent for economic or political access abroad to an accommodation with Chinese interests.

The task thus became to weaken the American-Japanese alliance, and at the same time, to prevent at all costs, a "forward" Japanese policy with respect to Korea or Taiwan. To this end, the Chinese leaders have conducted a massive political offensive, much of it aimed directly at the internal Japanese scene. They have wooed not merely Socialists, Democratic Socialists, and Komeito members, but they have reached deeply into the Liberal Democratic Party itself, encouraging each of the anti-Sato factions to engage in direct negotiations with Peking, and establish their own separate lines of communication. Similar approaches have been taken toward the Japanese business community; the labor union leadership; and the intellectuals, literati and journalists. With the olive branch extended in one hand, Peking has brandished the sword in the other, issuing a fiat to the Sato government that unless it is willing to accept unconditionally the principle that Taiwan is a part of the Chinese People's Republic, there can be no formal negotiations concerning a normalization of relations.

The Chinese campaign, a brilliant example of how a foreign state can enter the domestic political scene of an open society today, and of how inextricably connected have become domestic and international politics, has forced the Sato government currently onto the defensive. Indeed, Peking would appear to have a fair chance of achieving its major objectives with a post-Sato administration. If Peking can pressure Tokyo into a full acceptance of the Chinese position on Taiwan as the price for normalized relations and at the same time help her to move in the direction of accepting North Korea on terms roughly equal to those now accorded South Korea, it will have scored its greatest diplomatic victory since Mao and his followers achieved power in 1949. If, in addition, the drumfire campaign against "Japanese militarism" helps to keep Japan from pursuing the path now being followed by China, namely, the route to nuclear and conventional military power of formidable proportions, another gain will have been achieved.

If these developments should come to pass will China be able and willing in exchange to provide Japan with the economic opportunities, political support, and credible security guarantees to warrant to the Japanese the risks involved in such acceptance of Chinese terms for the future of Northeast Asia? No issue is likely to be more heatedly debated in the coming months than this. Irrespective of the immediate answers, moreover, one can assume that the question will recur periodically, given the evidences of political instability now present in both of these states, and the radical differences in economic stage of development, political values, and way of life that now separate them.

"China is our half-brother," is a common Japanese saying,

and one susceptible to quite different implications. The future of Japanese-Chinese relations remains uncertain, obscured by the great clouds that billow over the Asian political horizon. Most, if not all, of the objective factors would indicate that competiton rather than cooperation will dominate Sino-Japanese relations during the 1970s, and that these relations will be relatively minimal and marked by recurrent crises. If nationalism is a force with which to reckon in the new Japan, it is omnipresent in China, often in virulent form. Each of these nations now seeks a role beyond its present one, and with special reference to Asia. While their disparate strengths and systems might in some respects be conducive to a complementary relation, they are also conducive to minimal communications and serious friction, in part, over the continued involvement of China in internal Japanese politics. For Japan, the China problem will not be resolved quickly or easily.

Japanese-Soviet Relations

Relations between Japan and the Soviet Union are subject to inhibitions of a psychological-political nature quite different from those affecting Japanese-Chinese relations. If some Japanese have a guilt complex regarding China, coupled with a deep appreciation of Chinese culture and a feeling of relative comfortableness in the presence of Chinese (a sense of understanding that people and hence, of being unable to fear them), none of these feelings apply to the Russians. Japan regards herself as wronged by the Soviet Union, both at the close of World War II and during the long, harsh years that followed. Many Japanese have not forgotten the manner in which prisoners of war were treated, and the Carthaginian peace terms upon Japan which the Soviet Union wanted to impose. The Russians, moreover, are very foreign, with a culture that has limited appeal to the Japanese. Here, the union between foreignism and fear can be seen in its most graphic form.

Thus, historic enmity, profound cultural differences, and racial antipathies serve as obstacles to Japanese-Russian rapprochement. Public opinion polls, as we have seen, provide concrete evidence on this score, as do attitudes within the Japanese elite. The pressures upon the Japanese government to improve relations with the Soviet Union are consequently very limited in comparison with those arising over the China issue.

In point of fact, however, improved relations between Japan and the Soviet Union might well prove more meaningful to Japan at this point than improved relations with China. As we have noted, there are reasonable prospects for important economic ties, some of which might provide Japan with substantial quantities of raw materials and energy sources. Of at least equal importance is that for a nation desperately short of bargaining leverage with China, relations with Russia represent one potential weapon. Might Peking be prepared to make some concessions to prevent or moderate Soviet-Japanese collaboration on her northern frontiers?

If such a possibility exists, however, it also provides a restraint upon Japanese-Russian cooperation, as suggested earlier. How far can Japan go in expanding her relations with the Soviet Union, without antagonizing Peking and thereby provoking greater rigidity, adding to domestic as well as international complications for Japan? There is another risk to be weighed. Should Japan aid the Russians in the development of a major strategic complex in the north Pacific, close to Japanese as well as to Chinese territories? Clearly, assistance in the construction of harbor facilities, the expansion of pipelines, and the exploitation of oil and gas supplies aim in that direction.

Despite these dilemmas, the chances are reasonably good for an improvement in Japanese-Soviet relations, particularly if the Russians are prepared to make concessions on the four islands at the tip of the Kuriles which Japan regards as historically hers. To improve relations with Russia, in contrast to the case with China, requires few costs on the part of Japan at present, and promises greater immediate benefits, both economic and political. Japanese-Soviet relations, however, are likely to be characterized by a business-like atmosphere, involving a cool calculation by each side of its respective interests, and without intimacy and emotional fervor.

Japanese-American Ties

As Japan views the great triangle formed around her, there remains the United States, a nation with which for more than a quarter of a century she has been far more closely related than with any other foreign state in her entire history. Certain factors now operate to weaken the Japanese-American alliance. Doubts regarding reliability or credibility have arisen on both sides. In Japan, the earlier, strongly favorable image of the United States in the public mind has been tarnished — partly as a result of efforts by segments of the influential media and intelligentsia, where anti-Americanism has never been more in vogue. Above all, the Japanese have no desire to be tied to a faltering power, a leader that sometimes appears to lack the will to lead and under whom, in recent times, failures have been as conspicuous as successes. Perhaps more than most people, the Japanese want to be associated with success at this point.

These mainly subjective factors have helped to shape the new Japanese nationalism. So far, this nationalism is without a fixed political expression, available to any group on the political spectrum and used on occasion by everyone. Thus, an imprecise phrase like "autonomous diplomacy" can evoke near unanimous support, symbolizing as it does a commitment to reassert Japan's full independence and authority in the international arena, but binding the nation to no specific tasks, burdens, or risks.

There is a strong element of frustration among Japanese leaders at present, however, for while "subjective" factors are propelling Japan in the general direction of a more forceful, independent policy, "objective" factors are, for the most part, operating in a countervailing fashion. A bold opening to either China or Russia can have limited meaning at best, because the critical economic, political, and strategic factors that would underwrite it are largely absent. Equidistant diplomacy or neutralism suffers from similar liabilities, and pan-Asianism in any exclusive sense would be sheer madness.

Thus, barring some major disaster to America at home or abroad, Japan's own interests would appear to be best served by working within the broad perimeters of a policy already established, that of an alliance with the United States. As has been suggested, that alliance can be modified in a variety of ways: by moving away from an exclusive reliance upon bilateralism via a number of multilateral commitments and guarantees; by a broadening of diplomatic and economic contacts, including a normalization of relations with most, if not all Communist states; and by the use of economic power to defend wider Japanese interests, developing in the course of such use certain policies different from those of the United States. Increasingly, the term, "alliance" may become less appropriate than a looser term such as "special ties." U.S.-Japan relations, moreover, are likely to be affected more and more by a series of multilateral commitments that surround and interact with them. In economic affairs, as we have noted, such ties will be both with the "advanced"

Western world and the developing states. In the strategic arena, hopefully, multilateral agreements regarding arms reduction and control will encompass Communist and non-Communist states alike.

Nevertheless, if Japan chooses a nonmilitary approach in her quest for an international role and the protection of her interests, and seeks to rely mainly upon her economic power in these respects, the strategy of united front operations with the non-Communist developing states, particularly those of Asia, could have an increasing appeal. For the weak states of Asia, the choices in international politics are those of a client-patron relation, a gamble on neutralism, or some form of regional cooperation which may not go beyond the economic or political realm, but which represents an effort through aggregation to turn weakness into strength.

Current developments offer enhanced opportunities for regional political groupings of smaller states. In an increasingly multipolar world, such regional groups would be able to exercise meaningful political pressure upon the major actors, given the narrow and shifting power balances that will prevail. Under certain circumstances, indeed, such pressure might become crucial since power today involves access to the domestic political processes of a state in addition to sheer military capacity. To date, the great advantages in this respect have lain with the closed, authoritarian societies which have near-total control over internal communications and organization. It will become more difficult, however, to exclude completely the collective political pressure emanating from a regional group of states, especially neighboring states. Their role in an international forum like the United Nations would also be much more meaningful than that of a single adversary. Thus, an important new aspect of international politics may now be unfolding, one with special significance for Japan. Already, that nation has taken an active role in organizations like ASPAC (Asian and Pacific Council) and ASEAN (Association of Southeast Asian Nations).

It would be wise not to minimize the obstacles faced by Japan in this respect, however. The smaller states of Asia are aware of Japan's enormous economic power, and many of them fear Japanese domination. Hence, progress is likely to be slow, with opposition frequently encountered.

How will the United States react to the developments sketched above, and to the wider political alternatives presently confronting Japan? It scarcely need be said that it is extremely hazardous at this point to predict American attitudes and policies. We are in a period that is at once dangerous and promising, hopeful and potentially disastrous, and all of this is reflected in the uneasy, volatile public mood that currently dominates the American political landscape. Events could transpire in Asia that would thrust the United States ever more rapidly down the withdrawal route, and sharply reduce her credibility. Let us assume, however, that the broad premises upon which the Nixon Doctrine are based continue to be valid, and that the path now charted can be maintained.

In such an event, the United States would have every reason to support a modified alliance with Japan, one flexible enough to encompass both multilateral agreements that strengthened the prospects for international peace and regional groupings that increased the leverage of the smaller and nonnuclear states. In this fashion, burdens could be more widely shared and at the same time, the international political climate could be tested step by step, with "alliance" gradually transformed into "special ties" if conditions warranted such a development.

THE SECURITY DIMENSIONS IN U.S.-JAPANESE RELATIONS

Let us now turn specifically to the security issues as they affect U.S.-Japan relations. A formal end to the American Occupation of Japan came during the Korean War, at a time when relations between the then unified Communist bloc and the non-Communist allies led by the United States were extremely bad. The threat of a general war hung over both Asia and Europe. Thus, concurrently with the Treaty of San Francisco which reestablished Japan's full sovereignty (a treaty to which the Communist states refused to adhere), a Mutual Security Treaty was concluded. This treaty provided that the United States accept responsibility for the defense of Japan against any external attack (in exchange for base rights).

First concluded in 1951, the Mutual Security Treaty was reaffirmed after certain revisions in the spring of 1960, amidst unprecedented scenes of tumult and violence both in the Diet and in the streets. Ten years later in 1970, however, the treaty was automatically renewed without significant protest. Nevertheless, security issues between the United States and Japan, together with broader questions relating to the extent and nature of Japanese rearmament, and to what military role, if any, Japan should assume internationally, have continued to produce extensive division and debate.

Security Issues and the Japanese Public

Let us go directly to central issues. Does a threat exist to Japan's security, and if so, from whence does that threat come? In January 1969, in an *Asahi* survey, these questions were posed.[33] Of those answering, 32 percent stated that they felt a threat from another country existed while 52 percent responded negatively. Of those answering affirmatively, 15 percent cited China, 5 percent the Soviet Union, and 6 percent the United States.[34] At the same time, when respondents were asked whether they thought a war was likely to break out, only between 10-20 percent answered affirmatively, and 70-80 percent responded negatively, with the Socialists providing the bulk of the affirmative answers.

There has been no data subsequently that would contradict these results. The perception of external threat in Japan remains low, a powerful factor in influencing both public opinion and the views of the political elite concerning security policies.

Coupled with the issue of threat is that of response. In the event of an emergency, will the United States defend Japan? Periodically, this question has been put to the Japanese public, and the recent answers have been as follows:

	Yomiuri June '69	Central Research February '70	Yomiuri Oct. '71
No. of cases	(2,311)	(2,255)	(2,965)
U.S. will defend Japan	37%	30%	30%
U.S. will not	29	39	38
Don't know	34	31	32
	100%	**100%**	**100%**

If these polls are accurate, the Japanese people are deeply divided over the value of an American defense commitment. There is a similar division over the usefulness of American bases in Japan to that nation's peace and security. Thirty-eight percent of the respondents in 1969 considered them "rather" or "very" useful, but 41 percent asserted that they were either "not useful" or "harmful."[36] A plurality of Japanese (44%) queried, moreover, saw the primary purpose of such bases the protection of the United States, with only 13 percent viewing them as for the protection of Japan, and an additional 12 percent seeing them as for the protection of other Asian countries.[37] It is not surprising, therefore, that a large majority of Japanese have preferred to have United States bases either "reduced" (47%) or "removed completely" (22%), with only 19 percent supporting the status quo (18%) or expanded bases (1%).[38]

When asked in this same poll what was the best way to protect the peace and security of Japan, with only one answer being allowed, the results were as follows:[39]

No. of Cases	(1086)
Increase our own military strength	25%
Join a regional military group of non-Communist countries	6
Rely mostly on the United States	4
Rely mostly on the United Nations	11
Adopt a neutral policy	29
Don't know	24
No answer	1
	100%

As of 1969, at least, the Japanese people were sharply divided over the best means of protecting themselves, with the advocates of rearmament and neutralism nearly equal in numbers, and those prepared to rely primarily upon the United States few. However, a more recent poll centering upon the questions of defense expenditures produced the following results:[40]

	September 1971
Because economic strength has increased, defense strength should increase	18%
Because the economic burden is heavy, defense strength should not increase over and above present level	51 ⎫
Because of the weight of people's livelihood, defense strength should decrease	19 ⎬ 70%
Don't know/no answer	12 ⎭
	100%

It is thus apparent that electorate support for increases in defense expenditures is limited at this point. To be correlated with this are public attitudes concerning the role of Japan in Asia and in the world. Most Japanese apparently do not regard Japan as a "big power," and are relatively satisfied with this fact, preferring that Japan concentrate upon strengthening the country internally rather than upon assuming a leadership role internationally. A recent Japan Broadcasting Corporation (NHK) poll had some extremely interesting data on these points.[41]

Collectively, the data present a picture of an electorate divided and confused over the critical issues pertaining to defense policies, but in the main, reluctant to see Japan undertake any major foreign policy burdens or risks. Electorate opinion is susceptible to dramatic changes, we would reiterate, and in any case, it does not necessarily mirror the views of the political and economic elite. Here too, however, the divisions are currently sharp. It is not surprising, therefore, that the Diet debates over security issues in recent years have been acrimonious, and that on occasion the administration has been hard pressed to win approval for its policies. Nevertheless, in terms of expenditures, defense commitments have risen substantially in the past two decades, having increased at an average of 15-20 percent annually.

What have these expenditures produced? Today, Japan might be considered a middle-level military power, vastly inferior to the superpowers in every respect, and significantly below the military strength of such varied states as France, the People's Republic of China, and probably the two Koreas, but sometimes ranked seventh in the world roster of military powers. The premium is upon modernity, not size. Japan's Self-Defense Forces number less than 250,000 in all branches of service, with the army table of organization calling for 180,000 men. In equipment, the current emphasis is upon the newest tanks, armored cars and automatic weapons for the ground forces: advance trainers and Phantom fighters for the air force, together with such defensive weapons as surface-to-air missiles; and a wide range of naval fighting ships, including plans for helicopter-carrying aircraft carriers.

The 4th Defense Plan, originally scheduled for full implementation beginning July 1, 1972, called for a defense build-up which by 1976 would enable the SDF to cope with any "localized war," to maintain air supremacy over its own territory, and to control the neighboring seas "within the necessary boundaries." This plan originally called for an expenditure of Y5,800 billion ($2.6 billion) during the 1972-1976 period, with a Fiscal 1972 budget of Y803 billion, a 19.7% increase over the Fiscal 1971 defense budget. In the 1972 budget, however, only 38.8 percent of the increased expenditure was for new equipment, with more than 50 percent involved in increased personnel costs, primarily salary and fringe-benefit raises.

Final approval of the 4th Defense Plan has been delayed, and the 1972 defense budget was approved by the Diet only after a lengthy deadlock, and some compromises by the Sato administration. The government had initially attempted to secure passage of the new budget without having first obtained the approval of the National Defense Council. The opposition parties therefore sought to make "civilian control" an issue, and boycotted the Diet for nearly three weeks, illustrating once again the precarious working of the Japanese parliamentary system. The budget was ultimately approved with modest revisions, largely because on this issue, the Liberal Democratic Party remained united.

The longer range issues, however, remain unresolved, and at this point, it would be most accurate to assert that Japan is keeping her military options open, watching carefully developments in Asia and in the United States. Up to date, the Japanese government has done little to cultivate public opinion on behalf of its policies, one factor contributing to the generally negative public reaction to increased military spending. Meanwhile, factional leaders within the Liberal Democratic Party content themselves with support for limited, nonnuclear defense measures, opposing — at least for this period — any effort to revise Article 9 of the Constitution which is generally regarded as prohibiting the use of Japanese military forces overseas.

Currently, the government takes a strong stand against the development of nuclear weapons, proclaiming that it intends to pursue the three nonnuclear principles: nonproduction, nonpossession, and nonintroduction (of U.S. nuclear weapons onto Japanese soil). The last of these principles has resulted in periodic charges by the opposition that American nuclear weapons have been on Japanese soil secretly at points in the recent past (charges denied by the United States), and that the pledge to remove nuclear weapons from Okinawa at the time of its reversion to Japan cannot be trusted unless full inspection of American facilities is allowed.

The Nuclear Issue

The question of whether Japan will ultimately go nuclear continues to divide the outside world, and the Japanese people themselves. There can be little doubt about current Japanese views on whether nuclear weapons should be developed by their government. In the various polls that have been taken in recent years, three-fourths to two-thirds of the respondents have opposed the development of such weapons.[42] On the other hand, those believing that Japan will ultimately have nuclear weapons equal in numbers those who feel that Japan will never possess them.

On this, as on other matters, public opinion might prove fickle, depending upon events. But the arguments against the acquisition of nuclear weapons remain very persuasive in Japan. First, there are the simple geopolitical facts of life: Japan is a very small, highly congested nation, with over 100 million people crammed into a total land area less than that of California. A large number of them live in an almost solidly metropolitan stretch between Tokyo and Osaka-Kobe, on the east coast of Honshu. Under these conditions, a nuclear conflict would be particularly devastating — and the memories of Hiroshima and Nagasaki, when nuclear weapons were still in their infancy, are kept alive in many ways.

It can also be doubted that either Great Britain or France has acquired "great power" status or significantly increased political leverage from its possession of nuclear weapons. It is true, of course, that all of the nuclear powers are accorded some international status, including permanent membership in the United Nations. The latter fact, however, stems from decisions made when the U.N. was established, not from events during the nuclear era. There is very little evidence, meanwhile, to support the thesis that Great Britain or France have been able to use their nuclear club membership in highly effective ways politically or economically.

What are the arguments on the other side? It is sometimes asserted that as long as Japan is a nonnuclear power, she will have to pursue the politics of dependency. Coming under the American nuclear umbrella, or dependent upon the "good will" of Russia and China; Japan will never be able to establish a truly autonomous foreign policy, nor obtain a full hearing for her point of view, it is said. Those who advocate the acquisition of nuclear weapons regard the possibility of Japan's being involved in a full-fledged nuclear war as exceedingly remote, especially in any solo capacity. They believe, however, that the development of such weapons as nuclear powered submarines and tactical nuclear weapons is the only logical outcome of any major military modernization program. And they ask whether a purely conventional force — even with its numbers greatly expanded — can represent any meaningful defense against a nuclear power, hence, any asset in a bargaining negotiatory situation. On the other hand, even a limited nuclear capacity means the ability to wreak heavy damage on any opponent, therefore having some deterrent effect and providing some bargaining leverage.

From an economic standpoint, there are no barriers to a Japanese acquisition of nuclear weapons. Up to date, Japan has been spending less than one percent of her GNP on defense, a far smaller expenditure than that of any other major nation and most minor ones. The funds involved in a nuclear program would produce no adverse effect upon the Japanese economy. From a technological standpoint also, the path is open to nuclearization. Indeed, Japan is already placing heavy emphasis upon the development of nuclear power for peaceful purposes, regarding this as a potentially major source of her future energy needs. Many other recent developments in Japan, both military and nonmilitary, would facilitate a conversion to nuclear weapons if that decision were made. It should be noted, moreover, that among Japan's newest equipment are ships and airplanes fully capable of utilizing nuclear weapons.

The evidence suggests that at least some planners within the Japanese government currently aim at a policy of "nuclearization minus two," namely, a policy of making it possible for Japan to acquire nuclear weapons, if that decision is reached, in approximately two years. Even if this is correct, however, there is no indication that a majority of governmental or LDP leaders support nuclearization at this time. On the contrary, there are strong indications that *under present circumstances*, a sizeable majority of conservatives as well as those of other political persuasions, are opposed to making Japan a nuclear power.

What could alter the present situation? The most probable source of change would be a greatly increased perception of threat to Japan. Such a threat would most logically come from the People's Republic of China, or possibly, from the Soviet Union. Presumably, China will begin testing middle-range missiles at some point in the foreseeable future. Will this be coupled with any explosive issues? One issue has already emerged, namely, the question of sovereignty over the Senkaku islands. Japan is currently involved in a verbal dispute with both the governments of Peking and Taipei over these islands. Located between Okinawa and Taiwan, the Senkakus, which may have important offshore oil resources, are claimed by Japan to have always been in Japanese possession. On this point, there appears to be little internal disagreement. Fukuda Takeo, Foreign Minister, moreover, has asserted that after the reversion of Okinawa on May 15, 1972, Japanese coast guard units would patrol the Senkaku area to prevent foreign encroachment.

Meanwhile, with Okinawan reversion, thousands of Japanese SDF men have been sent there, together with F-104 aircraft, antisubmarine units, and missile batteries. Thus, the Japanese defense commitment has now extended southward to encompass all Japanese territory. Could the confrontation over the Senkaku islands become serious? Will other issues, possibly involving Taiwan or the Korean peninsula produce threats, real or imagined, and induce a change in public and elitist sentiment? These questions cannot be answered with any certainty, especially given the volatile, highly unpredictable nature of the Asian international situation.

A second possible source of change in Japanese opinion and policies would be the total loss of American credibility.

Such an event, to be sure, would be productive of several diametrically opposed reactions. A severe American defeat in Asia, or a drastic withdrawal from the region, as part of a shift toward isolation, would encourage a polarization of Japanese views. Both the advocates of a pacifist-neutralist course and those urging greater self-defense efforts, would probably gain ground. Any prediction of the outcome in such an event is hazardous, but the debate over the general direction of Japanese foreign policy would surely become intensified.

Meanwhile, Japan has not yet ratified the nuclear nonproliferation treaty which the government signed two years ago, although there is still hope that this will be accomplished shortly. So far, the opposition arguments have centered upon fears that inspection of nuclear facilities will result in the theft of industrial secrets and the thesis that the treaty represents a "big power" demarche upon all other nations. But the most significant message conveyed by this delay is that current Japanese leaders are reluctant to foreclose their options with respect to nuclear weapons.

American Policies on Security Questions

What is the official American view on these matters, and what are the prospects regarding those American policies that could affect Japanese security? Perhaps the most important fact is that to the Japanese, the United States has seemed ambivalent and unclear with respect to Japanese security policies, and more important, with respect to the broad course desirable for Japanese foreign policy. On the one hand, U.S. policy seems clearly opposed to any move on the part of Japan to acquire nuclear weapons. Both privately and publicly, American officials argue that such a development would greatly complicate international relations in Asia, would not be conducive to peace in the region, and would not produce greater security for Japan. Indeed, Japanese leaders believe that Americans have stressed these points in conversations with Chou En-lai in order to indicate to the Chinese the importance of a continuing American presence in East Asia.

At the same time, however, American officials have encouraged the assumption of greater Japanese responsibility for self-defense, including the acquisition of the most modern conventional weapons. On occasion, moreover, American policy has also seemed designed to induce Japan to accept some responsibilities for the security of those two small states closest to the Japanese homeland, the Republic of Korea and the Republic of China on Taiwan. Indeed, it is a common assumption among many Japanese that the United States would like Japan to take up the American role in Asia, or at least, in Northeast Asia. The Chinese leaders, as indicated earlier, have also been operating on that assumption, particularly since the Sato-Nixon Communiqué concerning Okinawa issued in 1969, when it was asserted that developments regarding the Republic of Korea and Taiwan did affect the security of Japan.

More recently, as we have noted, the Japanese government has appeared to move away from any policies that might indicate long-term commitments either to Taiwan or to South Korea, and various pressures have been mounted upon Japan to accept a radically different Northeast Asia than the one envisaged at the time of the Sato-Nixon communiqué.

The probabilities are that by 1975-1980, the United States will have given up all, or almost all of its fixed bases in East Asia, and established its major military complex in the mid-Pacific, using various islands in the Mariana and Marshall groups. Some naval facilities may be preserved whereby American warships can be serviced, but for the most part, the emphasis will be upon the bases of allies being maintained at a readiness state, and the development of a capacity for first-line self-defense among all nations with which the United States has ties. In conjunction with these moves, existing security treaties are likely to be revised, including that with Japan.

Anticipating these developments, several leaders within the Liberal Democratic Party have already begun to speak of the need for the revision of the Mutual Security Treaty. Various study groups within the LDP have established security policy as a major theme for future study, and it has been suggested that security treaty revision, together with the China problem, will constitute the chief issues to be settled in the post-Sato years.

When the evidence is assembled, it can be asserted that under present conditions, the odds are strongly against large-scale rearmament in Japan, the acquisition of nuclear weapons, or the assumption of military responsibilities beyond Japan's home territory. Between now and 1976, Japan will continue to develop a small, but highly modern defense force, spending no more than one percent of the GNP for these purposes. There will be no effort to amend the Constitution to permit the use of these forces abroad. Opposition to the development of nuclear weapons will continue to be both strong and conclusive. The options, however, will be kept open, with events pertaining to Asia and to the United States constituting variables of critical significance. But for the short run at least, the political-military equilibrium in Asia is more likely to be influenced by Japan's minimal role than by her maximal role, and most probably there will be much agonizing, indecision, and uncertainty before Japan's security policies and foreign policy perimeters are finally fixed for the years ahead.

SUMMARY

Since World War II, American-Japanese relations have been deeply affected by the international environment. That will continue to be true. Is it to be a broad détente, a grinding, laborious step by step movement away from hostilities, or a series of new crises? Can some understanding on critical issues like nuclear weapons be achieved, or will we see nuclear proliferation? The unfolding of developments regarding these and other issues will have a forceful impact upon the relations between our two nations.

Domestic political trends are also going to influence decisions in the field of foreign policy, including American-Japanese relations, in no small degree. The complete absence of consensus on such matters has long been a hallmark of the Japanese political scene. There is no sign of change. On the contrary, within the ranks of the "conservatives" themselves, differences on specific foreign policy issues have become more serious. In the United States as well, after more than one-quarter of a century of bipartisan foreign policy, consensus has been eroded, with resulting uncertainties on the horizon. Thus, elections or splits within the governing party could have an effect, even a drastic effect, upon policy.

Even after one has sought to factor these variables into the equation, the logic underwriting continued close ties between Japan and the United States appears to be exceedingly strong. On the economic front, our two nations will have relations of crucial import for the predictable future. Rarely, if ever, has economic intercourse between two advanced states been so extensive. If our economic relations are handled properly, moreover, the mutual benefits can scarcely be exaggerated. Already, American-Japanese economic interaction has abetted some of the most spectacular economic development and improvements in livelihood that mankind has witnessed. Yet the need for proper management is underlined by the wide range of problems these relations have produced reflecting structural differences between the economies of our two societies, the advent of a heightened economic competition in the international arena, and policy shortcomings of both parties.

It should be possible to deal with most of these problems constructively, containing if not solving them. Earlier, we set forth suggestions for certain measures that might be taken to stabilize and improve our economic relations, recognizing that some of the most significant action must be multilateral, not just bilateral. It is probably in the sphere of economic affairs that the most decisive moves affecting the total American-Japanese relationship can be taken in the next period.

If the quest for a broad equilibrium in Asia is to be successful, political relations between the United States and Japan are scarcely less important than those in the economic field. And once again, the logic of continuing close ties is great. We hold a series of mutual values and mutual interests. Both nations are striving to work on the frontiers of freedom, preserving and enhancing political openness, while at the same time dealing with the new problems introduced by rapid economic growth, relative affluence, and the communications revolution. Both nations have an interest in seeing openness preserved and expanded elsewhere, and in making the principles of peaceful coexistence work. Our common political interests so far outweigh our political differences.

These circumstances make a modified alliance the most meaningful policy for our two countries at this point in time. Both neutralism and pan-Asianism in any pure form represent highly unrealistic approaches to the contemporary world for Japan, hence policies that could only undermine Japan's basic foreign and domestic goals. Similarly, isolationism would merely increase the middle and long-range risks for the United States in an age of more, not less, independence among nations.

Modified alliance connotes a relationship flexible enough to accept both multilateralism and regionalism. It must also involve much closer consultation at official levels on the widest range of issues, with ample room for separate positions when that seems warranted. Our special ties, moreover, should be buttressed by an ever-widening circle of regular contacts at nonofficial levels.

It is truly ironic that at a time when the Chinese People's Republic is rapidly expanding its people-to-people diplomacy with Japan and the U.S. through semiofficial channels, the American and Japanese people still have relatively limited cultural, professional and political contacts on any regular or systematic basis. This is not to denigrate contacts with China. Yet it is obvious that the greatest fund of common interests and common problems currently exist between Americans and Japanese. Discussions at the private level, moreover, are all the more important given the rising interrelations between public-elite attitudes and foreign policies.

Fortunately, some promising steps are now being taken to improve this situation. The Japanese government is establishing a counterpart program to the Fulbright Program which should greatly facilitate contacts in the scholarly field. Business ties have always been the most substantial source for private communications, and continue to be of great importance. Labor has also maintained certain relations with its Japanese counterpart. At some point in the near future, therefore, a large network of semipermanent as well as *ad hoc* relationships may have woven influential segments of the American and Japanese community together, providing a basis for the refinement of attitudes and policies alike, and serving to direct as well as to strengthen governmental relations.

The broad direction of American strategic policies with respect to Asia seems now to have been charted. As indicated earlier, we shall increasingly remove our military forces from fixed bases in forward areas, and consider our primary defense line the mid-Pacific. Under the Nixon Doctrine, those nations with whom we have security commitments will be expected to handle their own first-line defense, under American nuclear protection, and with the possible use of American air and sea power in the event of overt aggression. If this position can be maintained, the American commitment should remain credible, precluding the need for Japan to develop nuclear weapons.

Thus far, however, we have been discussing the logic of close American-Japanese ties as if such matters were wholly determined by impersonal, rational considerations. In point of fact, the sharp deterioration of those relations in recent years has been caused in considerable part by human responses involving a high level of emotionalism in some cases. As we have emphasized, real issues between us have emerged. Nor is there any desire here to deny logic totally to alternative policies and courses of action. It remains a basic fact, however, that the atmosphere of distrust and suspicion at elitist levels, gradually reflected at the citizenry level, is the single most ominous trend of the last several years.

It is entirely possible that our relations could be poisoned, all logic notwithstanding, if we cannot establish trust and understanding as individuals and groups, creating the institutions that will foster such a trend. Events of recent years serve to indicate that despite our many common interests, we do spring from very different cultures, with different modes of behavior and different ways of thought. An acceptance of difference — and an understanding of it — are thus as important as an acceptance of mutuality. Once again, a network of personal and private group ties interacting with official relations can be helpful.

Thus, nothing can be taken for granted concerning American-Japanese relations in the future. It should be acknowledged that continued deterioration is possible. But it would be subjective feelings as much or more than objective differences that would cause such deterioration. If each party will remember this, we may now be able to construct a better foundation for a relationship that remains critical to both of us.

NOTES

1. Ohira Masayoshi, "The Shaking World and Japan," *Jiyu (Liberty)*, January, 1972, pp. 112-127 (p.117) All Japanese names in this monograph are presented in Japanese fashion, family names preceding given name.
2. Council on Industrial Structure of Japan, "Trade and Industry Policies in the 1970's" May 1971, Tokyo, p.1.
3. A speech of Ushiba Nobuhiko, Ambassador of Japan to the United States, January 10, 1972, Commonwealth Club, San Francisco.
4. "Industrial Review of Japan, 1972" *The Japan Economic Journal (Nihon Keizai Shimbun)*, December 1971, Tokyo, p.11.
5. An American scholar who has done much to refine our understanding of the relationship between government and business in Japan is William W. Lockwood. See his *The Economic Development of Japan*, Princeton, 1954, and "Japan's 'New Capitalism,' " in a work edited by him, *The State and Economic Enterprise in Japan*, Princeton, 1965.
6. For recent American evaluations of the sources of post-1945 Japanese economic growth and current trends within the Japanese economy, see United States Foreign Economic Policy of the Committee on Foreign Affairs, House of Representatives, 92nd Congress, First Session, Nov. 2,3,4, and 8, 1971, U.S. Government Printing Office, Washington, D.C., 1972.

   In Japanese, see Kato, Yasuo, *Sengo Nihon no Kodo seicho to junkan (High Growth and Cycles of the Postwar Economy)*, Tokyo: Miraisha, 1967, 246 pp.

   Nakayama, Ichiro, ed., *Nihon keizai no seicho — Kodo seicho o sasaeru mono, (Japanese Economic Growth — Factors to Support High Economic Growth)*, Tokyo University Press, 1960, 295 pp.

   Nenji Keizai hokoku (Annual Economic Report), Tokyo: Keizai Kikakucho [some issues are also called *Keizai hakusho*] (*Economic White Papers*).

   Shinohara Miyohei, *Keizai seicho no kozo (Structure*

of Economic Growth), Tokyo, Kokugen Shobo, 1964, 272 pp.

7. *The Japan Economic Review*, February 15, 1972, p. 4.

8. Trends in 1971, as already suggested, were particularly volatile from a political standpoint. Japanese exports to the United States increased over the previous year by 26.5 percent, and accounted for 31.2 percent of Japan's total exports in value for that year. The major item accounting for this increase was a 43.5 percent increase in machinery exports, the bulk of which were automobiles. Machinery accounted for approximately 54 percent of all U.S. imports from Japan. Meanwhile, due to the business recession in Japan and other factors, Japanese imports from the U.S. in 1971 were 10.5 percent less than in 1970 — which contrasted with an average growth rate of some 18.6 percent for the 1965-1970 period. "Finance Ministry Bares Value of Japan's Trade in '71," *Economic News from Japan*, Economic Affairs Bureau, Ministry of Foreign Affairs, Tokyo, February-March 1972, p. 6.

For two additional Japanese surveys from different perspectives, see Okita Saburo, "Meeting a New Situation with Respect to Japanese-American Economic Relations, *Nihon Keizai Kenkyu Center*, No. 155, July 1, 1971, pp. 2-7, and a symposium on "The Road to Adjusting Japanese-American Economic Relations," *Shukan Toyo Keizai*, July 31, 1971, pp. 32-40.

9. For a comprehensive analysis of Chinese issue up to the beginning of 1971 from a Japanese moderate point of view, see Shimada Takemitsu, "China and Japanese-American Relations," *Sekai Shuho*, January 1, 1971, pp. 16-27.

10. According to Soviet sources, the oil reserves in the Tyumen oil field total between 30 and 40 billion tons, and the Russians would be able to supply Japan with between 25 and 40 million tons annually. Currently, Japan depends upon the Middle East for more than 90 percent of its crude oil requirements.

The project would involve the strengthening of existing pipelines between Tyumen and Irkutsk, and the building of new lines from Irkutsk to Nakhodka, on the Pacific Ocean. When completed, these lines would be more than 7,700 kilometers in length, constituting the longest pipeline in the world. For recent details, see "Japan Survey Mission Going to Siberia to Probe Projects for Oil, Natural Gas," *The Japan Economic Review*, March 15, 1972, p. 3.

See also "The Background of Gromyko's Visit to Japan," in *Sekai* (The World), No. 316, March, 1972, pp. 171-174.

1. Japanese trade with the European Economic Community has been scarcely one-fifth that with the United States in recent years, although recently, EEC trade has been increasing at a rapid percentage rate. EEC spokesmen insist that the reasons for the low trade have lain essentially in natural economic conditions: geography, Japanese concentration upon the more prosperous and unified American market, and the sharper competition faced by Japanese products in Europe. See Commission of European Communities, *Information Memo*, "Commercial Relations between Japan, the United States and the European Community," Mimeographed, Brussels, April 1972.

While these factors unquestionably play an important role in restraining trade, EEC restrictions upon Japanese trade are not unimportant, especially those pertaining to transhipment within the Community. Moreover, EEC-Japan trade negotiations are completely stalled at present. In the wake of the Nixon administration's economic moves, the Europeans fear a flood of Japanese exports, and want a tight safeguard clause in any agreement, a stipulation being resisted by Japan.

2. In an article entitled "The American View of Japan," *Kokusai Mondai*, (The International World), November, 1970, Miyamoto Nobuo of the Planning Division, Research and Analysis Department, Ministry of Foreign Affairs, characterized the dual nature of the Japanese as follows: quarrelsome but meek; militaristic but aesthetic; arrogant but well mannered; stubborn but adaptable;

obedient but resentful of being pushed around; brave but cowards; conservative but prepared to welcome change.

Japanese writers, it might be noted, often seem to have a preoccupation with introspection, and are frequently more harsh on themselves than would seem warranted. One does not need to accept these particular characterizations, nor regard contradictory traits as unique to this culture alone, however, to be struck by the strong elements of contrast that enter into Japanese political thought and behavior, rendering any analysis of probable actions and role the more hazardous.

13. The data cited here comes from a poll taken for the United States Information Agency by Central Research Services, Inc., between September 1 and 15, 1969, based on interviews with a national probability sample of 1,086 adults. The results do not differ significantly, however, from those obtained by other polls.

14. This poll is published in USIA, *Research Memorandum*, October 27, 1971. Many other Japanese polls are available through USIA Research Memoranda.

15. Those Japanese (48%) who saw some deterioration in U.S.-Japanese relations as likely to occur, cited the following reasons:

From a trade/economic standpoint, the U.S. is
making various demands of Japan   28%
The competition resulting from Japan's increasing
economic strength   22%
The U.S. is pursuing its diplomatic course without
considering Japan's position   16%
From a military standpoint, the U.S. is making
various demands upon Japan   13%
Considering its own position, Japan is adopting
an independent policy   9%
As Japan's defense ability is strengthened, the need
for U.S. assistance is gradually reduced   6%
Not asked (had expressed view that friendly
relations would continue, or gave no opinion) 52%

16. The poll was published in *Asahi*, January 3, 1972, p. 1 and 7, with the full results being as follows:

	Sept. 1969	Nov. 1970	May 1971	Dec. 1971
United States	40%	42%	39%	28%
People's Republic of China	10	21	21	33
Republic of Korea	1	1	0	0
Soviet Union	2	3	4	1
North Korea	0	0	1	1
Other Asian Nations	4	3	3	3
Other Nations	1	1	1	1
All Nations	28	6	7	5
Other answers	4	3	2	3
No answer[1]	10	20	22	25
	100%	100%	100%	100%

[1] Includes both those not answering and those stating that they did not know.

17. In the *Asahi* poll of December 1971, when asked, Which party do you like best? the results were as follows:

Date of Poll	Liberal Democratic Party	Inclined to LDP	Japan Socialist Party	Inclined to JSP	Komeito	Inclined to Komeito
Dec. '71	32	10	18	9	4	1
Nov. '70	40	9	18	7	3	1
Dec. '68	40	8	21	6	4	1
Aug. '65	38	7	27	7	3	1
Aug. '62	36	12	23	8	–	–

Date of Poll	Democratic Socialist Party	Inclined to DSP	Japan Communist Party	Inclined to JCP	No Answer
Dec. '71	6	2	4	1	13
Nov. '70	5	2	4	1	10
Dec. '68	6	2	1	1	10
Aug. '65	3	1	1	0	12
Aug. '62	3	1	1	0	16

18. "Policies for the 1972 Movement," *Shakaito (The Socialist Party)*, No. 181 March 1972, p. 74.
19. *Ibid.*, pp. 75-76
20. See *Shakai Shimpo (The Socialist News)*, January 23, 1972, p. 1., for Kawasaki's statement.

21. *Ibid.,* p. 1. Other similar statements are readily available. On November 1, 1971, at the conclusion of the 5th official Socialist Party mission to China led by party chairman Narita Tomomi, a joint communiqué was issued condemning "U.S. imperialism" as "the enemy of the world," a phrase first accepted by Asanuma Inejiro a decade ago, and asserting that the people of Asia were facing the joint threat of "U.S. imperialism working together with Japanese militarism." The communiqué pledged a combined struggle on the part of the people of Japan, China, Korea and Indochina against these forces. While these themes too had been advanced in earlier communiqués, on this occasion, reference to "the four enemies" previously cited, namely, "U.S. imperialism," the "reactionary" Sato government, Soviet "revisionism," and the Japanese Communist "revisionists" under Miyamoto Kenji, was omitted.

22. Hakamada Satomi (vice-chairman of the JCP Politburo), "The Issues of Political Renovation and the Advance of Our Party," *Zenei,* (*Vanguard*), January 1972, p. 14.

23. *Akahata* (*Red Flag*), April 5, 1972, p. 1.

24. "Concerning the Nixon visit to China and the Sino-U.S. Joint Communiqué," A Statement by the Japan Communist Party Foreign Policy Committee," *Ibid.*, February 29, 1972, p. 1.

25. Hakamada, *op. cit.*, p. 12

26. "Interview with Chairman Takeiri Before His Visit to the United States: Will Have Serious and Frank Discussion with the U.S.," *Komei Shimbun,* (*The Komei News*) March 10, 1972, p. 1.

27. Editorial, "The Transition to an Autonomous Foreign Policy to be Pursued," *Komei,* January 1972, p. 13.
    See also an interview with Yano Junya (secretary of the Komeito), entitled, "Victory in the Councillor Elections and Future Political Directions," *Ibid.*, August 1971, pp. 65-66.

28. Kamijo Sueo, "Changes in the Basic Policies of the Democratic Socialist Party," *Kaikakusha,* (A *Reformed Society*), January 1972, p. 51.

29. For the recent views of certain factional leaders within the Liberal Democratic Party on foreign policy, see the following articles: Fukuda Takeo, "Japanese Foreign Policy from Now — We Do Not Choose the Road of a Militarist Big Power," *Ajicho Geppo*, (*Asian Survey Monthly*), March 1972, pp. 2-13; Ohira Masayoshi, "The Various Problems which Surround Japan," *Ibid.*, February 1972, pp. 30-41; and Miki Takeo, "The Political Topics of This Year", *Jiyu,* April 1972, pp. 123-127.

30. For a view reflecting the attitudes of those within the LDP seeking "better relations" with China, see Tagawa Seiichi, "Basic Viewpoints on the Japan-China Problem," *Economist*, August 24, 1972, pp. 28-33.

31. For articles reflective of the "reformist" currents, see Kono Yohei, "Agreeing with the 'LDP Dissolution Theory'," *Bungei Shunju* (*Spring and Autumn Literature*), January 1972, pp. 144-151; and Yamazaki Masakazu and Kono Yohei, "Politics Writing the Second Act," Jiyu, May 1972, pp. 154-168.

It should be noted that the above authors are relatively young LDP Diet members, not destined for top power. The men expected to inaugurate new leadership trends in the 1970s are individuals like Tanaka and Nakasone. Some able observers, it should be stated, do not believe that generational differences are significant, and are inclined to doubt that any major changes will occur, at least during the coming decade. They feel that the men most likely to follow Sato have already been coopted into the system, and that — given the financial considerations involved in Japanese politics — the business community will continue to block effectively any break-away tendencies with the Liberal Democratic Party, demanding party unification as the price for continued monetary support. This view has merit. The issue is primarily a question of degree, namely, to what extent, and with what timing will Japan's dominant party evolve toward a new political style accompanied by certain alternations in policies. In any case, it is unlikely that such changes will occur in an exceedingly rapid or highly dramatic form.

32. It should be noted, however, that it was a Japanese journalist, Miyoshi Osamu, who first exposed this extraordinary case. Writing in the April 1972 *Keizai Orai*, (Economic Correspondence), Miyoshi charged that *Asahi*, *Nihon Keizai, Nishi Nippon* and the Kyodo News Agency, using intermediaries, had accepted three conditions imposed by the Chinese government for the stationing of their newsmen in Peking: no support for "the plot" to create two Chinas or one China, one Taiwan; no undermining of efforts to improve Japan-China (C.P.R.) relations; and no "hostile" reporting on the People's Republic of China. These conditions, asserted Miyoshi, first laid down in 1964, and reiterated when the agreement on newsmen was revised in 1968, were tacitly accepted, although the agreement did not come in written form.

    Several of the principals involved subsequently admitted that these facts were correct in interviews with Sam Jameson of the *Los Angeles Times*. Tagawa, Seiichi, LDP Diet member, confirmed that he had participated in the initial discussions with Peking, as did Ejiri Susumu, Secretary-General of the Japan Newspaper Publishers Association. Kawamura Kenji, foreign editor of *Asahi*, defended the agreement saying, "We had already agreed to them (the three principles) in our editorials."!

    See the *Los Angeles Times*, April 14, 1972, pp. 1, 26-28. For an earlier analysis of press bias, see Irie Michimasa, "The Mass Media is Dancing to the Tune of the China Problem," *Jiyu* (*Liberty*), May 1971, pp.28-35.33.

33. This poll is cited by Wantanabe Akio, "Reversion of Okinawa: the Changing U.S.-Japan Alliance," *Chuo Koron*, August 1971.

34. It should be noted that as of 1969, the majority of Japanese saw the basic interests of Japan as in agreement with those of the United States. Fifty-three percent saw the basic interests of Japan and the United States as either "very much" (5%) or "fairly well" (48%) in agreement — a gain over the 38% in 1965. Only 15%

believed that the basic interests of the two countries differ. In marked constrast, a majority of Japanese (56%) viewed the Soviet Union's basic interests as "rather" (33%) or "very" (23%) different from those of Japan. A scant 6% saw the basic interests of the two countreis as fairly well in agreement and less than 1% saw them as very much in agreement. A near majority (48%) saw Japanese and Chinese interests as different, and only 7% saw them as in agreement. A modified national probability sample of 1,086 adults conducted for the USIA by Central Research Service, Inc., between September 1-16, 1969.

35. USIA *Research Memorandum*, October 22, 1971, p. 1. Since exactly the same wording was not used in the three surveys, some variation in opinion might be attributed to this.

36. USIA, Office of Research and Assessment, "The American Domestic Scene and the U.S. Presence in Japan," A report based upon interviews conducted for the Agency by Central Research Services, Inc., between September 1 and 15, 1969. Publication dated June 26, 1970, p. 17.

37. *Ibid*.

38. *Ibid*.

39. *Ibid*., p. 18.

40. This poll was conducted by the Japan Broadcasting Corporation on September 26-27, 1971, among a general population sample of 2,523. It is reproduced in USIA, *Research Memorandum*, October 27, 1971, p. 3.

    Unfortunately, like many Japanese surveys, the questions here do not provide the respondent with neutrally worded, mutually exclusive options, and hence, the figures should be treated as trends rather than as precise measurement.

41. Note the following results from the September 1971 poll, published in *Ibid*., p. 2

	September 1971
Think Japan is a big power	34%
Do not think so	44
Can't say in general	14
Don't know/no answer	8
	100%

A majority (56%) prefer Japan to strengthen itself internally rather than seek to assume a leading international role:

"Here are two views:

(A) Japan should assume a leadership role, strengthening its voice internationally.

(B) Japan should concentrate on strengthening the country internally, rather than assuming leadership role internationally.

With which view do you agree more?"

	NHK September 1971	
View closer to A	20%	34%
Inclined toward A	14%	
Inclined toward B	25%	56%
View closer to B	31%	
Don't know/no answer	10%	
	100%	

42. Note the following poll data on this subject:

	August 1971
No. of cases	(936)
Possession of nuclear weapons is desirable	14%
Possession of nuclear weapons is undesirable	73
Can't say/don't know	13
	100%

Recent trend data from surveys of eligible Tokyo voters conducted by the Institute of Statistical Mathematics also show predominant opposition to the possession of nuclear weapons:

	1968 Spring (649)	1969 Spring (692)	1970 Spring (655)	1971 Spring (677)
Japan should never equip itself with nuclear weapons	56%	50%	57%	59%
[Acquiring nuclear weapons] is unavoidable under certain	33	40	30	31
circumstances	33	40	30	31
Other	2	2	2	1
Don't know	9	8	11	9
	100%	100%	100%	100%

The first poll presented above was conducted by *Sankei Shimbun*, a leading Japanese newspaper. The results were similar to those of a *Yomiuri Shimbun* poll of May 1970 which found that 8 percent considered it either "very" (3%) or "somewhat" (5%) desirable for Japan to have nuclear weapons, as opposed to 67 percent who considered it "somewhat" (22%) or "very" (45%) undesirable for Japan to acquire such weapons.

These polls are reproduced in USIA, Research Memorandum, December 21, 1971, p. 2.